TOMMY MURPHY was born in 1979 in Queanbeyan, the seventh of eight children. He is a graduate of the National Institute of Dramatic Art (Director's course) and the University of Sydney where he was president of Sydney University Dramatic Society.

He was winner of the Sydney Theatre Company Young Playwrights' Award and the ACT Young Writers' Award for his first play, *For God, Queen and Country*. His second play *Troy's House* was performed at SUDS, Australian Theatre for Young People, The Old Fitzroy, the Queanbeyan Bicentennial Centre and La Mama. *Strangers in Between* and *Holding the Man* were commissioned, developed and premiered by the Griffin Theatre Company where Tommy was in residence. *Strangers in Between* won the 2006 NSW Premier's Literary Award for Best Play.

Other works include an adaptation of Marlowe's *Massacre at Paris* (ATYP), a one-act play *Try Hard* (NIDA) and two collaborations for the 2002 Sydney Festival, *360 Positions in a One Night Stand* (Kicking and Screaming Theatre) and *Kinderspiel* (ATYP and Theater an der Parkaue, Berlin).

Strangers in Between

Holding the Man

Adapted from the book by Timothy Conigrave

Two plays by

TOMMY MURPHY

Currency Press, Sydney

CURRENCY PLAYS

First published in 2006
by Currency Press Pty Ltd,
PO Box 2287, Strawberry Hills, NSW, 2012, Australia
enquiries@currency.com.au
www.currency.com.au

In accordance with the requirement of the Australian Media, Entertainment & Arts
Alliance, Currency Press has made every effort to identify, and gain permission of,
the artists who appear in the photographs which illustrate these plays.

NATIONAL LIBRARY OF AUSTRALIA CIP DATA

Murphy, Tommy.
    Strangers in between; &, Holding the man.
    ISBN 9780868197968 (pbk.).
    ISBN 0 86819 796 3 (pbk.).
    I. Conigrave, Timothy, 1959-1994. Holding the man. II.
    Title. III. Title : Holding the man (Play).
A822.4

Australian Government

Australia Council
for the Arts

Publication of this title was assisted by
the Commonwealth Government through
the Australia Council, its arts funding and
advisory body.

Set by Matt Applewhite.
Cover design by Kate Florance, Currency Press.
Printed by Hyde Park Press, Adelaide.

Front cover: Sam Dunn in the Griffin Theatre Company production of *Strangers in
Between*, 2005. Photo: Michael Corridore.
Author photo: Prudence Murphy.

Contents

A Theatre of Optimism

David Berthold   *vii*

Acknowledgements   *xiii*

STRANGERS IN BETWEEN   1

    Act One   5

    Act Two   39

HOLDING THE MAN   65

    Act One   69

    Act Two   115

A Theatre of Optimism

David Berthold

Tommy Murphy is an optimist, and writes comedies. We experience this optimism in the seductive, theatrical buoyancy of the storytelling. *Strangers in Between* and *Holding the Man* take us into the heart of darkness, but they do so with an affirming flame and a relish for living.

The plays thrive on delicious situations, the delightfully characteristic, and a good joke. They are effortlessly inventive—not to show off, but as a means of sharing the joy of the story. I have never seen Tommy cry in a rehearsal room, except with laughter.

Strangers in Between was our sixth association, and *Holding the Man* our seventh. Our first was when, as Associate Director of Sydney Theatre Company, I had the task of directing a one-day workshop and reading of the winning play of the 1997 STC Young Playwrights' Award. Tommy arrived at the Wharf as a 16-year-old Queanbeyan Catholic schoolboy eager to see his play made flesh. One of the lines from that play remains one of the funniest I've ever heard.

A couple of years later Tommy directed his second play, *Troy's House*, for Sydney University Dramatic Society. I had just become Artistic Director of the Australian Theatre for Young People, so thought that if the play was good, I might direct a new production. It was the final SUDS performance. By the interval, I knew that the play was a small wonder. Its story of a group of teenagers at the end of their schooling was breathtakingly honest, ingenious, insightful, full of love, and a whole heap of fun. There was a clear magic in what Tommy had created with his fellow students, and I knew I could never do a better production. I invited the whole show over to ATYP's home at the Wharf, where it played an extra twelve sold-out performances. Tommy and I subsequently enjoyed several more projects at ATYP before coming together at Griffin where *Strangers in Between* and *Holding the Man* were produced in consecutive years.

Strangers in Between is about two brothers; *Holding the Man* about two male lovers. Both explore how men get on, and how alternative families are formed. More fundamentally, they ask why we hurt the very ones we love, and how that hurt might be healed.

The hurt in *Strangers* is a deep and mysterious one. Shane is sixteen, and has run away to Sydney's Kings Cross from his home in regional NSW because Ben, his older brother, beat him up. Ben caught Shane kissing a mate from school, a 15-year-old boy, and reacted with extreme violence. Shane spends much of the play trying to work out what has made Ben 'psycho'.

Shane is full of fear in Kings Cross. He is without family, and without the life and social skills necessary to get on in such an environment. This is a source of a great deal of inspired comedy. But it also makes us aware of how lucky Shane is to meet the two caring men who, separately, find themselves drawn into his life.

Will is a young urban guy, completely at ease with his sexuality. Peter is an older man, and rather lonely. Both relationships break down when sex is confused with intimacy, and when Shane reacts violently to both men, much as his brother reacted to him. Shane responds homophobic rage when Will tells him he needs to be tested for genital warts. Later, when Shane seeks solace with Peter, and both begin to enjoy (perhaps unwisely) a conversation that moves from erotic fantasy to physical contact, Shane snaps. He becomes his brother, accusing Peter of being a pervert and calculating predator.

At this point Ben makes a surprise entrance, and the play takes a turn. The ghost that Shane senses is a portent of Ben's arrival. Shane longs for his older brother to come and find him, and, it becomes increasingly clear to us, his imagination answers this need. We also see that the same actor plays Will and Ben for an important reason: Will is the form of Shane's yearning for Ben.

These are complex, fascinating scenes. On one level, Shane uses these conversations with Ben in order to hear what he wants to hear— news of home, that his parents are looking for him, that he is missed, and so on. On another level, Shane's desire for home and the need to understand and forgive his brother, to work out the source of his violence, is made manifest by Ben trying to draw him back to Goulburn with a promise of a visit to the pool. Somewhere in his subconscious Shane knows that the pool holds the key. The truth, as Shane imagines it (and he is probably right), emerges bit by bit, tantalisingly, with splashes of easing comedy, and Ben as unknowing puppet.

This imagined truth is the critical event lurking in the shadows. Though Shane barely remembers it, he witnessed an incident some years earlier, when Ben, a champion swimmer, was felt up by his coach Reg. It is only after Shane has worked out that Ben's fear is greater than his own, and without foundation, that he can go to the hospital to have his warts burnt off. Here, the play effortlessly slides between realities. Ben and Will morph, time curves, and we find ourselves in Peter's bathroom, post-hospital, all three men together for the first time since their initial chance meeting.

This final, hopeful scene is beautifully configured. On one level, this is a new family for Shane—Will as brother, Peter as mother. He sees Will for what he is, not as a form of Ben. Peter, too, finds a new family—his mother's funeral approaches and Shane is allowed to adopt a comforting role. For all three, familial intimacy has replaced sexual desire. On a symbolic level, this scene heals that dark, determining moment back at the pool: a soothing bath has replaced a threatening pool, Peter is a positive version of the paedophilic Reg, and Will is Ben reconciled. In the final, fragile moments Shane decides he will call his birth family. Tenderness and the desire to heal have replaced fear and the desire to hurt.

The design of the original production aimed towards this final scene. A bathroom setting playfully served for the earlier scenes: why not bathroom as bottle shop, with drinks found in the bath like at a party, or bathroom as laundromat? For all except the final scene, the bathroom was askew in some way, with the toilet in the wrong place (moveable, actually), various props in strange places, and so on. Then, as Shane woke from his post-hospital haze into the hands of his new family, the bathroom was finally and perfectly a bathroom, spotless and functional. The design seemed to reflect Shane's state of mind, with wit.

Hospital looms in *Holding the Man*, too, but this is a different world, not the stuff of genital warts. I suggested to Tommy that he take on the daunting task of adapting Timothy Conigrave's memoir in mid-2005. We had casually spoken of the book as play before we began *Strangers*, around Easter 2004, but at that stage neither of us, for different reasons, was confident enough to genuinely take hold of the idea. In fact, Tommy hadn't read the book. I was certainly aware of the colossal responsibility any adaptation would bear.

I first read the book when it was published in 1995—the day it hit the bookshops. I bought it on my way to the airport to catch an international flight. I read the book in one go, as many people have, and found myself blubbering over the last fifty pages or so, as many people have. My fellow passengers must have thought I'd lost it. I had read a few of the early chapters in manuscript form thanks to my friendship with Nick Enright, who shaped and edited much of the book, and so knew some of what to expect, yet the physical impact was a bombshell.

The book is wonderfully more than the sum of its parts. It has magic. This made it a dangerous prospect for any adaptation. Would we be able to retain that mysterious thing that made the magic? After the success of *Strangers*, I asked Tommy if he thought the book could make a play, and if he thought he was the playwright for the job. I knew he was, but wanted him to say it. I wasn't going to ask another writer if he said no. I gave him the book to read and a few days later his response came in the form of a very long and very personal letter. He read the book on a bus journey home to Queanbeyan, spellbound. Reading the book, he said, was like reading his own life, even though he was of a different generation and had no experience of HIV/AIDS. He read the final chapters with his head in his boyfriend's lap, sobbing. He wanted to make the play, for Tim.

We had to ask a lot of questions. Why should the book be a play? What part of the story do we concentrate on? What does AIDS mean on stage now?

The idea to adapt emerged, at the simplest level, because of the story's connection with Griffin Theatre Company. Tim was involved with the company during the mid-1980s, most notably as instigator of the *Soft Targets* project (Australia's first theatrical response to HIV/AIDS), and several episodes in the book were set at Griffin, one even on the Stables stage itself. This theatrical connection provided a way in: the play could release the theatre inherent in the book. After all, Tim was an actor and playwright, not a novelist, and the book was partly shaped by another playwright. Tellingly, in early letters to his publisher Tim calls sections of the book 'scenes'.

This observation suggested a *way* to tell the story, but *what* story? Part of Tim's reason for writing the book was to educate about HIV/ AIDS, but that was not our purpose here. We wanted the love story. We were particularly interested in the question: 'Why do we hurt the ones we love?' Tim hurt John repeatedly during their fifteen years together, and John absorbed the hurt. In story terms, AIDS might be seen as a metaphor, the final hurt. In story terms, it makes sense that Tim might have infected John.

Tommy's adaptation plays with theatre, taking joy in its possibilities. It begins with Tim and Damien as audience to a puppet Neil Armstrong, before zooming backstage at a shopping-centre version of *The Wizard of Oz*. Then to *Romeo and Juliet*, a love story and tragedy. Before too long, we're at Tim's NIDA audition, with the audition monologue seamlessly transforming into a crucial duologue with John. Three years at NIDA are dealt with in the form of a NIDA movement piece. A speech from the Stables stage has particular charm (especially in the first production). A research interview for *Soft Targets* gives us a second puppet, a representation of AIDS, a kind of grim reaper. The workshop of Tim's play *Thieving Boy* provides a holding mechanism for representing the forest of madness Tim experiences when he develops AIDS. John will give over his diminishing body to a third puppet.

The story is also partly told through gifts and documents. Throughout the play there are letters, newspapers, scripts, scrapbooks. John gives Tim several gifts in the play, and one of those, at the end of Act One, is a scrapbook telling the story of their first five years together. Tim gives John one defining gift, the central document, the book called *Holding the Man*, the story of their fifteen years together. In the play, we witness the moment when the decision to write the book is made—when John gives Tim a document holder at their hospital Christmas. Tim begins to remember, to shape their story together. We have come to believe that Tim wrote the book partly to say sorry (for all the hurt) and thank you (for all the love). Maybe that's why he writes John so idealistically, and himself so judgementally. The play is able to make a point of this.

Tommy's adaptation is a masterpiece of economy. Tim adjusted the raw material of his life to meet his storytelling needs, and Tommy has adjusted the source material of the book to meet his theatrical needs. Characters have been omitted and others conflated. Most notably, Phoebe in the play is a fusion of several characters in the book, and so she's been given a new name. Details from various episodes in the book have found their way into single scenes in the play. Somehow, Tommy has managed to retain the full sweep of the book, and through some conjuring trick we don't see what's missing.

It's also a work of great heart and wit. Tommy shares a few things with Tim, and two of these are a sparkling sense of humour and an ability to be astonishingly, but disarmingly candid. Maybe it's this mix, combined with the example of unconditional love and superhuman endurance, which gives this story its magic. I think Tommy has caught the mix, and managed to make the story both completely faithful to Tim's and yet wholly his own. It's a very significant achievement.

These two plays are from a writer at the beginning of his career, but in charge of his art. Tommy believes in theatre, and it shows. It makes his work a pleasure to produce and a joy to watch. These plays acknowledge the pain, but elevate the wonder, make the familiar strange and the strange familiar, and invite us to understand what belonging is. They are spoken in a brilliantly inventive vernacular through authentic characters that become our sons, our best friends, our lovers, and our parents. They leave us wanting more of their charm, their wisdom and, above all, their buoyant optimism.

David Berthold was the Artistic Director of Griffin Theatre Company, 2003–06. He directed the original productions of both Strangers in Between *and* Holding the Man. *He was Artistic Director of the Australian Theatre for Young People (1999–2003), Associate Director of Sydney Theatre Company (1994–99) and Artistic Associate of Queensland Theatre Company (1991–93). He has also directed for Playbox, NIDA, La Boite, Opera Queensland, Auckland Theatre Company, the National Theatre, London and Theater an der Parkaue, Berlin.*

Acknowledgements

Tommy Murphy

I am indebted to Griffin Theatre Company for the support and respect offered to emerging playwrights. David Berthold's visionary artistic directorship and his establishment of a Playwright's Residency gave me a home and access to an exhilarating stage. It has been an honour to see my work performed at that legendary diamond, wedged between its eager audience, the SBW Stables.

I gratefully acknowledge everyone who contributed to the development, production and publication of these plays including Michael 'Mica' Agosta, Arts NSW, Beth Aubrey, Alice Babidge, Alison Barnes, Anthony Blair, Mary Rachel Brown, Simon Burke, Director of the Lowy Institute HIV/AIDS Project Bill Bowtell, Cameron Creswell Management, Sadie Chrestman, Stephen Collins, Jeanette Cronin, Glenn Dulihanty, Sam Dunn, Nicholas Eadie, Guy Edmonds, Special Collections Archivist Academy Library ADFA Wilgha Edwards for the use of Nick Enright's archives, the Vincent Fairfax Family Foundation, Gadens Lawyers, Charlie Garber, Anthony Gee, Ben Gerrard, Debbie Golvan, Head of the HIV Epidemiology and Prevention Program Associate Professor Andrew Grulich, Sheridan Harbridge, Amy Hardingham, Stephen Hawker, Basil Hogios, Garth Holcombe, Ros Horin, Chris Hurrell, Gunnar Isaacson, Ed Kavalee, Tony Knight, NIDA Archivist Margaret Leask, Sharne Macdonald and RGM, Hetty Marriott Brittan, Graham 'Hazards' Maxwell, Nathan McIlroy, Spencer McLaren, Robin McLeavy, Aubrey Mellor, Eve Morey, Martin Murphy, Paddy Murphy, Prudence Murphy, Hugh O'Keefe, Courtney O'Regan, Debra Oswald, Anthony Pearson, Anthony Phelan, Laura Pike, the Ian Potter Foundation, Clare Rainbow, Nicole Robinson, Kristian Schmid, Jim Sharman, Brett Stiller, Christopher Stollery, Brian Thomson, Cain Thompson, James Waites, Xavier College, William Yang, Matt Zeremes, the Griffin staff and board, my peers and teachers at NIDA, my partner Dane Crawford and my family.

For *Holding the Man,* there were many people who shared their memories and love of Tim and John. They include Anna Davison, Dick, Mary-Gert and Nicholas Conigrave, James Bean, Penny Cook, Peter Craig, Sophie Cunningham, Franco Dechiera, Nellie Flannery, Elizabeth Gentle, Paul Goddard, Tim Jones, Peter Kingston, Victoria Longley, Brent Mackie, Craig Moore, Nicholas Papademetriou, Meredith Rose at Penguin, Morna Seres, David Thompson a Xavier school teacher, Pepe Trevor, Mark Trevorrow and Tracey Williams. My sincere thanks to all those who contributed in some way or another to my adaptation including those who were yet to do so at the time of publication.

♦ ♦ ♦ ♦ ♦

Strangers in Between

For Hugh

Sam Dunn as Shane and Brett Stiller as Will in the Griffin Theatre Company production of STRANGERS IN BETWEEN, 2005. (Photo: Robert McFarlane)

Strangers in Between was first produced by the Griffin Theatre Company at the SBW Stables Theatre, Sydney, on 11 February 2005, with the following cast:

SHANE	Sam Dunn
WILL / BEN	Brett Stiller
PETER	Anthony Phelan

Director, David Berthold
Designer, Alice Babidge
Lighting Designer, Anthony Pearson

CHARACTERS

SHANE, sixteen, but may appear older
WILL, early twenties
PETER, fifty to sixty
BEN, early twenties, Shane's brother

Casting Note
The same actor plays both Will and Ben.
Shane's physical description of Will on page 34–5 is part fantasy.

ACT ONE

A bottlo on the strip. SHANE *is at work.*

SHANE *is beautiful but he doesn't know it. He has been left alone for the first time.*

He adjusts bottles. He dusts. He flops the duster around and loses himself in his thoughts.

SHANE: [*to himself*] G'day. Hello. Do you need a hand? Good evening. G'day. Good evening. Is it cold out? G'day. Evening. Fuck, you make me laugh—let's go for coffee...

      WILL *enters unnoticed by* SHANE.

... I'll close up shop.

WILL: Are you closing?

SHANE: Hey? Oh no. Evening.

WILL: Hi.

SHANE: Do you need a hand?

WILL: Nah, just grabbing some grog.

SHANE: Let me know if you need a hand.

WILL: Thanks. [*Selecting a drink*] Um...

SHANE: What type of grog do you like?

WILL: All of it.

SHANE: Well, maybe you should get a selection.

WILL: Oh no. I'll just get this.

      WILL *selects some fancy pre-mixed bottles.*

SHANE: Good choice. Let me take that to the register for you.

WILL: I'm right.

SHANE: Cool. This way. Um. Okay. 'Vodka Black Ice.' I think there's a button for that. Six-pack?

WILL: Four-pack.

SHANE: Four-pack of Vodka Black Ice. No. I can't see the button for it.

WILL: Maybe you scan it.

SHANE: No. No, I think there's a button. Do you know how much it is?

WILL: About seven or eight bucks.

SHANE: Is it?

WILL: Nup. Let me check.

SHANE: Oh no. I'll check. I have to learn the prices. It's twelve ninety-five.

WILL: Cool.

SHANE: Twelve ninety-five? Is that a rip-off?

WILL: No. I mean, they're like six-fifty each in a bar.

SHANE: Really? Sounds like a rip-off to me. Okay. Twelve ninety-five.

>   SHANE *examines the cash register.*

Oh, how does this thing work?

WILL: They usually scan it.

SHANE: Oh, have you been here before?

WILL: Yeah, heaps.

SHANE: Oh, okay. Let's see. I thought I typed in the prices or something.

>   SHANE *scans the drinks.*

Oh yeah, no, that's right. It must be the wines I have a button for. You'd think there'd be a button for these too because buttons are easier, hey.

WILL: Yeah.

>   SHANE *is waiting for the register to open.*

SHANE: I might practise scanning stuff later.

WILL: Cool.

SHANE: Ooh, hang on. I'd have to clear each sale, wouldn't I?

WILL: I wouldn't know.

SHANE: Yeah. Now it hasn't opened. I thought the register just opened when you scan it.

WILL: I want to pay with EFTPOS anyway.

SHANE: Oh Jesus. You haven't got cash?

WILL: Just shrapnel.

SHANE: The manager will be back soon. Do you mind waiting a second?

WILL: Oh, I kind of have to go.

SHANE: Oh, okay. I don't know how to open the register, that's all. Why did he, ohhh. I mean, why did he leave me here? I can't do this. I've been here one day. This isn't even my shirt. My name's not Michelle.

SHANE's *shirt is embroidered with the name 'Michelle'.*

I mean, this is… look, I'm really sorry. Err.

SHANE *checks his pockets.*

I don't have… how much is it? Yeah, see, I don't have any change in my pocket.

WILL: Oh, that's okay. I'll just wait.

SHANE: He won't be long.

WILL: Cool.

SHANE: Sorry, hey.

WILL: So you've just started here?

SHANE: Yeah. Yesterday. I worked next door before that.

WILL: Maccas?

SHANE: Yeah. Just for a week.

WILL: Right. And is it good here?

SHANE: Well, yeah, I think so. Um, some of the guys are arseholes. The manager's a bit of a cock. He just thinks I'm so dumb.

PETER *enters.*

WILL: Is this him?

SHANE: No. I don't know who this is. [*to* PETER] Evening. Do you need a hand?

PETER: Oh well, that's good service. Just looking for a wine.

SHANE: Can I help you?

PETER: Oh yes, well, I think so. Just in the market for a reasonable chardonnay, I think.

SHANE: Red or white?

PETER: [*winking*] Let's try white.

SHANE: Okay then.

PETER: Keep it cheap and cheerful. Just off to a family thing.

SHANE: These are our whites here.

PETER: Good. So what do you recommend?

SHANE: Oh, yeah. They're all good.

PETER: Mmmh, yes, no need for it to be good per se. It's not like they'll know, bless them.

SHANE: That looks cheap.

PETER: Perhaps cheaper I think. Although, I like that drop. I'll grab that one for my brother-in-law and me. Now, for my sister... Do you have Queen Adelaide?

SHANE: Um. I don't know.

PETER: Could get her a cask...

SHANE: There. There's Queen Adelaide.

PETER: Well spotted.

SHANE: Cool.

PETER *selects a bottle.*

PETER: And how are you boys tonight?

SHANE: Good.

PETER: It's a lovely evening.

SHANE: Yeah.

PETER: Just gorgeous.

SHANE: How much for those? Do they say on them?

PETER: Thirteen ninety-five and six fifty.

SHANE: Okay. Nineteen dollars forty-five...

WILL: Twenty.

SHANE: No. Yes. Twenty forty-five, thanks.

PETER: Bargain. Thank you.

PETER *hands over a twenty and a five-dollar note.*

SHANE: You don't have the exact?

PETER: Sorry.

WILL *retrieves the change in his pocket.*

SHANE: Okay...

WILL: Hang on. [*to* PETER] Here you are. There's four dollars and, hang on, fifty-five cents.

PETER: Thanking you.

PETER *touches* WILL's *hand as he takes the money.*

WILL: [*to* SHANE] You can pay me back when the register's opened.

SHANE: Oh, okay.

PETER: Cheerio, boys.

SHANE: Bye, have a nice day... night.

PETER *exits.*

WILL: Yuck, old sleaze.

SHANE: What do you mean?

WILL: See how he looked at us?

SHANE: No.

WILL: Yeah, so gross. As if.

SHANE: Yeah.

WILL: I'm never going to be like that. And all that stuff about their families: Get over it.

SHANE: Yeah.

WILL: So, are you going out after this?

SHANE: Oh, I don't know. Probably not.

WILL: Oh, right.

SHANE: You?

WILL: Yeah, I might. I mean, yeah, no, I definitely am. I'm just going to dinner at my friends' and then yeah, we're going out to get trashed.

SHANE: Where's good to go around here?

WILL: Are you from out of town?

SHANE: I've just moved here from Goulburn.

WILL: Oh right. Do you like it here?

SHANE: It's better than Goulburn.

WILL: What's wrong with Goulburn?

SHANE: I had to get out. It's better here. It's just better not knowing people. Everyone thinks they know everything about everyone in Goulburn.

WILL: Yeah. No Big Banana here but. That's what you've got, isn't it?

SHANE: A Big Merino actually. You've got a big Coke sign but. That's good.

WILL: Yeah, guess so. And there's stuff to do in the Cross which is also good, I guess. Still, must be fun to live in the country with all those... actually, no, it would suck. It's good you moved. Better then hanging out and hanging yourself or whatever young guys do there. Do you need someone to show you around?

SHANE: Yeah. Cool.

WILL: So what time do you finish?

SHANE: I finish in like half an hour but I can't tonight. I've gotta wait to get paid.

WILL: Oh well, maybe later in the week.

SHANE: Excellent, yeah.

WILL: Do you have a phone number?

SHANE: We have one here. I don't know what it is but. You could look it up or just come and see me. I'm working three hours every night this week except tomorrow. I usually start at five.

WILL: Okay then. I'll pop in.

SHANE: Cool. You're not a backpacker murderer or anything, are you?

WILL: Hey? Um… Are you a backpacker?

SHANE: No. No, I mean, you're not dodgy?

WILL: No.

SHANE: I know you're not. I could tell as soon as you came in. You've gotta be alert but. There's no alarm here. Some people try to steal stuff. I can tell. I'm just going to let them but. They might have needles.

WILL: Yeah. But you'll be all right.

SHANE: Do you wanna just take these? Make it cost the nine dollars and fifty-five cents that you gave that gross guy. I'll make it work out when the manager comes back.

WILL: You sure?

SHANE: He's probably just smoking pot out the back. He'll be stoned. It's fine.

WILL: Cool. Thanks heaps.

SHANE: Yeah.

WILL: Cool. Bye Michelle.

SHANE: Yeah, nah, it's Shane.

WILL: I'm Will.

SHANE: Cool. Bye Will.

WILL: Bye.

♦ ♦ ♦ ♦ ♦

The Bourbon and Beefsteak. A day or two later.

SHANE *finds a table. He has a plate of oily nibblies in front of him; a spring roll, a cocktail frankfurt, some corn chips and a mini meat pie.* PETER *is nearby at another table.*

SHANE: Excuse me. Do you know how much longer they have the free bar snacks out for?

PETER: Just for happy hour.

SHANE: How long's that for?

PETER: Another hour and a half.

SHANE: Cool. You go to my bottlo, hey.

PETER: Oh, do I? Which one is that?

SHANE: The one next to Maccas.

PETER: Oh yes. You served me last week. I remember. The register was on the blink.

SHANE: Yeah. That's right. You got the Queen Adelaide.

PETER: I don't think so.

SHANE: Yeah, I'm learning all the names of them.

PETER: Good, I would have got the Rosemount. Hang on, no, I bought something nasty for my sister. She hated that.

SHANE: Oh right. Yeah, the Rosemount's cheap too. But not actually cheap. They're all expensive. Wine's just pricey.

PETER *drinks.*

I've never been here before. This is good, hey. Do you know how much the beefsteak is?

PETER: There's a menu there.

SHANE: Cool.

SHANE *holds up a Bourbon and Beefsteak menu.*

I might sit at your table.

PETER: I'm waiting for…

SHANE *sits at* PETER*'s table.*

SHANE: I like this place.

PETER: Yes. It's good.

Silence.

We call it 'the office'.

SHANE: What?

PETER: This place. My friend Graeme and I call it 'the office'. We're forever saying, 'I'll meet you at the office.' He's meant to be here now but he's held up at some hellish godchild's birthday party. He wanted moral support but I said, 'Pass the bloody parcel, I don't think so. I simply can't pull myself away from the office.' Was very funny.

SHANE: Oh right. [*Finishing reading the menu*] Man! As if you'd order any of that when they give you free stuff.

PETER: Right, well, I think they want you to order a drink too.

SHANE: What a 'bourbon'? I got a glass of water.

PETER: Goodo.

SHANE: So do you live around here?

PETER: Yes.

SHANE: Yeah, it's dodgy, hey.

PETER: I've never had any trouble.

SHANE: Really? A girl got acid thrown on her face just near my house.

PETER: Isn't that dreadful?

SHANE: Yeah. Probably drug-related.

PETER: Maybe.

SHANE: Yeah. Do you want me to get you a plate of snacks?

PETER: Oh no. I'm fine. Yes, I quite like living amongst all this. I walk home past the prostitutes and the bikies and the junkies and somehow I feel at home.

SHANE: So what do you do?

PETER: Oh, I work for the government.

Sam Dunn as Shane and Anthony Phelan as Peter in the Griffin Theatre Company production of STRANGERS IN BETWEEN, 2005. (Photo: Robert McFarlane)

SHANE: As a what?

PETER: In one of their departments. Roads. Main roads. I'm the head trainer in HR. It's all a bit boring. But I draw. That's my interesting side.

SHANE: Awesome. What do you draw?

PETER: Still life.

SHANE: Nude people.

PETER: No, pots and domestic things.

SHANE: Cool. I did art at school.

PETER: Oh yeah.

SHANE: Yeah, but the teacher sucked and it was a bludge.

PETER: Oh well.

SHANE: Hey, can I ask you something?

PETER: I think so.

SHANE: Are you meant to keep honey in the fridge?

PETER: Oh.

SHANE: That's just something I've needed to ask someone.

PETER: No, you don't have to. It goes hard if you do.

SHANE: Oh. Yeah, I'm keeping it on a shelf—on a little bookshelf—but I didn't know if you're meant to or not. I won't put it in the fridge.

PETER: No, it's hard to spread.

SHANE: Yeah, as long as it won't go off.

PETER: No.

SHANE: Good. I don't have a fridge and I love honey. What about fabric softener?

PETER: On a shelf is fine.

SHANE: But do you have to use it?

PETER: No.

SHANE: Right. But if you do use it, do you have to use laundry powder as well?

PETER: Oh yes. It won't clean your clothes. It will just soften them.

SHANE: I thought as much.

PETER: Do you use powder or liquid?

SHANE: Um…

PETER: Powder is cheaper but liquid is better.

SHANE: Oh. Look, I just cleaned them in my sink but my room smells like damp, I think. I just used this soap stuff I bought. It's too chalky but.

PETER: Yeah, look, grab a bottle of liquid. Maybe you should go to a laundromat.

SHANE: I thought about that but how do you start? Do you just walk in with a bag of clothes?

PETER: Yes.

SHANE: Right.

PETER: It's fairly cheap.

SHANE: Is it? And like, you just go in? You don't ring them first or anything?

PETER: No.

SHANE: Cool. I might do that.

PETER: Are you fresh out of home?

SHANE: You can tell, hey. I don't fit in around here, hey. Everyone's a freak, hey. Not you. I didn't mean you're a freak.

PETER: That's okay.

SHANE: Yeah, you don't look like a Kings Cross person. Everyone around here looks like the guys who run dodgem cars at the show.

PETER: Oh, they're all right.

SHANE: Carnies? No they're not. Only time people lock up their homes in Goulburn's when the show's in town.

PETER: Is that right?

SHANE: Yep. I reckon everyone locks their door all the time around here but. You must feel a bit, you know—living here, you must feel like, you're like surrounded by freaks. Do you?

PETER: Yes but I love it.

SHANE: I don't love it. I think it's friggin' ugly.

PETER: It just came back from the war a little bit mad. That's what I say. I've lived here for years and I love it. I walk home past the prostitutes and the bikies and the junkies and somehow I feel very at home.

SHANE: Yeah, you said that.

PETER: Am I repeating myself?

SHANE: Yeah but that's okay.

PETER: Must be time for another wine.

> PETER *pours another glass from a bottle of white wine in a cooler next to the table. He also has two cans of VB.*

Would you like one of these?

SHANE: I'm sweet.

PETER: No, go on. I can't work out happy hour to save my life. I asked for one wine and here I am with a bottle and two cans of VB. I can't drink all this myself.

SHANE: Really? Oh, okay but I'm a bit of a Cadbury. I might just take one home.

PETER: They're already open.

SHANE: Oh. Okay.

PETER: Happy times.

SHANE: Cheers.

They drink.

PETER: Now, I do like your hair.

SHANE: Oh nah. It was cheap. I think my hairdresser's a junkie.

PETER: I think it looks 'cool'.

SHANE: Thanks.

PETER: I'm Peter by the way.

SHANE: I'm Shane.

SHANE *extends his hand to shake.*

PETER: How do you do, Shane?

SHANE: Good.

PETER: Gorgeous.

SHANE: Cool. Hey, look, Peter… I'm really sorry but I won't be able to shout you back a drink.

PETER: That's all right, mate.

SHANE: I would but I bought a toasted-sandwich maker yesterday and like…

PETER: Don't mention it.

SHANE: Cool. Just as long as you know.

PETER: Yes.

SHANE: Peter, you wouldn't be able to walk me home after this, could ya?

PETER: Oh, well…

SHANE: I just live like down there. I'm not like a drug user or anything.

PETER: I know.

SHANE: Cool. I'm not dodgy.

PETER: I know you're not.

SHANE: As long as you know that.

PETER: Look at your skin. Isn't it beautiful?

SHANE: Oh no, it's not.

PETER: No, it's so soft.

SHANE: I have heaps of pimples.

PETER: Where?

SHANE: Oh, everywhere. In my T-zone.

PETER: What's your T-zone?

SHANE: [*indicating a horizontal line above his eyes and a vertical one down the centre of his face*] It's here and here. It's my problem area.

PETER: Fuckin' pimples. Too funny. I'd trade a few things for pimples.

SHANE: And I noticed this the other day. If I squint. See?

PETER: What?

SHANE: Crows' nests or whatever.

PETER: Please.

SHANE: And my squint is lopsided.

PETER: Oh, for goodness' sake.

SHANE: It's true. My face has changed.

PETER: I'm surprised they let you in here.

SHANE: Why? I'm nineteen. Do they ID here?

PETER: I've never been asked.

SHANE: But maybe they'll card me. I mean, I am nineteen. I just left my licence in my flat. I'm on my blacks and everything.

PETER: Don't worry. You look nineteen.

SHANE: Do I?

PETER: Well, sixteen at a push.

SHANE: Oh shit. Do you think so?

PETER: Drink up. It will be fine. I make you look older anyhow. No one too young would be drinking with this old thing. I might have to get you to walk me home. I left my walking frame by the Smokey Dawson chair so I'll need an arm to lean on.

SHANE: Do you have a walking frame?

PETER: No. I was joking.

SHANE: Oh right. I can walk you home if you want.

PETER: Oh, Graeme'd love this. We'll see how we go.

SHANE: So how old are you?

PETER: Old enough. I don't do birthdays any more.

SHANE: Why not?

PETER: Because the last one was spent in a sauna.

SHANE: Why in a sauna?

PETER: Never mind.

SHANE: Hey, see that woman over there?

PETER: Where?

SHANE: Across the road.

PETER: Oh yes.

SHANE: I think she might be a prostitute.

PETER: Yes, she is.

SHANE: Oh. Right. There you go, hey.

PETER: Why did you want me to walk you home, Shane?

SHANE: No reason.

PETER: Did you want me to see where you live?

SHANE: No.

PETER: I could come over if you want.

SHANE: Oh no, it's too messy for visitors. I just wanted someone to walk home with.

PETER: I understand.

SHANE: Yeah, I just get… You know.

PETER: What?

SHANE: I just get scared around here sometimes. I'm scared I'll get beaten up or something. I've heard of like gangs and stuff that smash people for fun. That happens in Sydney.

PETER: Not around here. They'd mug you for your phone here.

SHANE: Yeah, see? That's fucked. I don't have a phone but that's fucked. I'm scared of that. I'm getting streetwise but. I never walk through parks and I walk in the middle of the road so you can see people jumping out of bushes.

PETER: As long as you don't get hit by a car.

SHANE: That's better than being beaten up. At least in Goulburn people punch your head in because they know you. I hate Sydney sometimes.

PETER: It's actually fine. You don't have to be paranoid.

SHANE: Yeah, well, I've known violent people, like my brother, he's full on and I… Violent people scare me. And all the junkies around here look like friggin' zombies and it's fucked. I saw one fully bleeding from the head before without knowing it. That's so fucked.

PETER: Well, that's no good.

SHANE: And it's just tonight 'cause I didn't work today and I just sat around by myself doin' bugger all. That's why I'm so glad I met you because I reckon if I went another day not talking to someone properly I'd fuckin' die. I was meant to see this guy—this guy I served at the bottlo—but his phone always goes to voicemail. I'm a bit weird in Sydney… I mean, I'm just babbling on to you without letting you talk. I'd never do that in Goulburn.

PETER: Well, I've never been to Goulburn.

SHANE: Oh, haven't ya? It's where that guy is.

PETER: Right.

SHANE: In the gaol. The murderer. The famous one.

PETER: I don't know.

SHANE: I want to say Ivan Henjak but he used to play in the Canberra Raiders and it's not him.

PETER: Right.

SHANE: Anyway, I'm from Goulburn too. I like to talk. Not just think. You know how you see things—just little things—that you would mention to another person. Like the shape my sheets made the 'smorning looked like the map of Australia. I had no one to tell that to, you know?

PETER: Where were the Snowy Mountains?

SHANE: What?

PETER: Nothing. You going to drink that or just hold it?

SHANE: Oh yeah. I don't drink beer much.

PETER: Have some wine.

SHANE: That's okay. You're actually not supposed to accept drinks from strangers anyway.

PETER: Oh well, I'm okay.

SHANE: Yeah, I know. [*He drinks.*] Ivan Milat. That's his name.

PETER: The backpacker murderer?

SHANE: Yeah. He's in Goulburn. They have him in this room, which is like suspended by chains and they have microphones around it to listen for filing or digging. They reckon his only motive is to get out now. That's all he thinks about.

PETER: Probably a few people who feel that way in Goulburn.

SHANE: Milat not Ivan Henjak. Do you like rugby league?

PETER: I buy the calendars.

SHANE: Oh right. Yeah, I don't like it any more. I don't know what I like any more. Everything's changing.

PETER: You don't like eating alone.

SHANE: Nup.

PETER: But this isn't your meal, is it?

SHANE: What?

PETER: The bar snacks.

SHANE: Oh. Yeah but I normally eat better.

PETER: Are you sure?

SHANE: Yeah. I had salad the other night. After I was coming back from this guy's house. The guy I met. The guy I served at the bottlo. Just this guy. I had this nice like pink salad from one of those shops on the main street bit here.

PETER: Like a seafood salad? I don't think they'd be very nourishing, young man. You'll have to come over for dinner.

SHANE: Really?

PETER: Yes. I'd love to cook for you.

SHANE: Cool. I'd love to let you.

PETER: Good. I cooked for my sister last week. She was visiting and it was simply hell. I'd take more care for you. I wouldn't deliberately use too much chilli. That sort of thing. What do you like to eat?

SHANE: I don't know.

PETER: I'd love to make a terrine. I read about terrines the other day. They're back.

SHANE: Cool. I don't know what that is.

PETER: It'll be a meat-cake thing. It's nice. Yes, I think I will do that.

SHANE: Cool. So why do you hate your sister?

PETER: Well, I don't hate her. I just think she's a bit of a pain in the arse. We've just been arranging some things and she's a moron. She can't help it.

SHANE: Is she the favourite? My brother was always the favourite.

PETER: Oh well, she probably was actually but my parents aren't around any more so it's not like that.

SHANE: Did they die?

PETER: Dad did. Mum's in a home now.

SHANE: Do you visit her much?

PETER: Well, she's in Adelaide. So it's pretty hard…

SHANE: Why?

PETER: She's completely dependent on nurses. She has to be lifted and washed. I'd be of no use to her. She's just not there any more.

SHANE: That's bad.

PETER: Have you ever been to a nursing home?

SHANE: No.

PETER: I've only been once—truth be known. Mum doesn't know because she doesn't know anything nowadays so… but I went in when she was first admitted… It smells like shit and there's all these desperate voices calling for nurses. Heavens above. And my sister was being all ridiculous and calling Mum 'dear' like she was the adult and Mum was a bloody toddler. And I saw the nurses lifting her onto this thing to be washed and I thought, hello, I can't do this. I just cannot do this.

SHANE: That must suck, hey.

PETER: But tell me about this boy you met.

SHANE: Oh, it sounds like I'm a poof or something?

PETER: Oh. Aren't you?

SHANE: Hey? Do you think I'm poofy?

PETER: Oh no. Not if you aren't. You were just going on about him and I thought you might be together but that's okay.

SHANE: Yeah, I'm not. It's just 'cause I'm in Sydney. It's made me a bit of a girl. I've been noticing my voice is higher. I can't explain it.

PETER: Probably just excitement.

SHANE: Yeah. So this guy…

PETER: Yes.

SHANE: Well, I met him. I served him at the bottlo. When you came in. He gave me the money. He and I, you know, hooked up. Yeah and he's really nice. We have heaps of fun. He says funny things. I want to think of something funny he said but I can't.

PETER: Sounds nice.

SHANE: It's okay to be gay here, hey.

PETER: Oh, it's okay anywhere.

SHANE: Not in Goulburn. There wasn't one other gay person in Goulburn. Sorry, actually of course there was. Joel Cochrane was the only one… and me but I'm not gay. I'm not full-blown gay. I'm just… in Sydney. I reckon all the gay people from all the little towns come here.

PETER: Well, maybe. I escaped from Adelaide after all.

SHANE: Really? Are you gay?

PETER: Well. Yeah.
SHANE: Oh.
PETER: You don't have to sit further away.
SHANE: No, I wasn't. I'm gay. I'm gay too.
PETER: Good.
SHANE: That's the first time I've said that.
PETER: Really?
SHANE: I've never said those words to anyone.
PETER: Feels good, doesn't it?
SHANE: Yeah. I mean, I'm probably bi.
PETER: Whatever, it doesn't matter.
SHANE: Yeah, I like girls and boys. Man, I know people who would
smash me if they heard that.
PETER: Like who?
SHANE: Most people.
PETER: Your brother?
SHANE: Everyone.
PETER: Well, they're not here. Cheers.
SHANE: Cheers.

They drink.

Can I ask you something?
PETER: Yes.
SHANE: You know coathangers?
PETER: Yes.
SHANE: Where do you get them from?
PETER: I don't know.
SHANE: Yeah, there isn't a shop for them. Everyone just has them, hey.
Especially the wire ones and they're the ones I want. I reckon if I
hung my clothes they wouldn't smell damp.
PETER: I'm always throwing coathangers out. They must just grow. I'll
give you some to start a crop.
SHANE: Oh. Okay. Thanks, Peter.

Pause.

So, how do you have anal sex? I tried the other night but it didn't
work. It just didn't fit. I was able to do it to him but.
PETER: Oh…

♦ ♦ ♦ ♦ ♦

SHANE*'s bedroom in a boarding house. Two or three weeks later.*

SHANE *has answered the door to* WILL.

SHANE: Fuck! Hi.

WILL: Oh, hi Shane.

SHANE: You scared me, hey. You knock really hard.

WILL: Sorry. How are you?

SHANE: Really good. Come in. This is cool. Jeez, it's been ages. I'm so glad I finally got on to ya.

WILL: Yeah, well, I couldn't return your messages.

SHANE: Yeah, I know. I'm getting a phone soon. Sorry, I probably left way too many messages on yours. I bet I sounded dumber and dumber each time.

WILL: No. It's fine.

SHANE: So this is where I live. It's not like your place. Take a seat.

WILL: Ta.

SHANE: I wish I had a chair to offer you.

WILL: No, that's fine.

　　　WILL *sits on the bed.*

SHANE: Yeah, I'm probably going to get a chair... From a second-hand place or something. I want like a nice wood one. I might make one.

WILL: Cool.

SHANE: Hey, I was thinking about cooking some soup.

WILL: Where?

SHANE: There's a microwave under you there.

WILL: Oh.

SHANE: My friend gave it to me.

　　　SHANE *retrieves a tin of soup.*

WILL: I won't eat. I thought we could go and get a coffee or something. We could eat at a café or something if you want.

SHANE: Oh cool. Yeah, I never go to caffs or anything. Let's hang out here for two more secs and then we'll go. Is that good?

WILL: Yep.

SHANE: I haven't really had anyone over yet.

WILL: Haven't ya?

SHANE: Na. Your pants are excellent.

WILL: They're new.

SHANE: Cool.

WILL: Yours are great too.

SHANE: No, these are old. They're too baggy. Baggy pants suck now. I want ones with zippers and all those pockets. Do you use that many pockets?

WILL: Nah.

SHANE: That's excellent.

WILL: Yeah.

SHANE: I'm close to the train station, hey.

WILL: Yeah. It's good.

SHANE: Yeah. What's that? Is that you knocking?

WILL: Yeah, I was just tapping my hand.

SHANE: Oh, that's okay. I thought it was something. Sometimes it creaks in here. I think it's haunted.

WILL: [*referring to a light shining through the window*] Does that light keep you up?

SHANE: No. I'm going to get a blind but. People walking down those stairs can see right in. I'm scared they might break in if they saw my alarm clock or something. Did those guys that sit at the station give you a hard time?

WILL: No.

SHANE: Sometimes they say stuff.

WILL: Nup.

SHANE: It's dangerous around here.

WILL: I've never had any trouble.

SHANE: I haven't either but I'm a bit 'you know' walking around. I think I'm going to buy a cricket bat. I saw a kid-sized one at one of them povo second-hand shops. 'Cause it is fully dodgy. A woman killed her baby with a hose at one of the houses near here.

WILL: How?

SHANE: Oh, in a bucket or something.

WILL: Shit.

SHANE: Yeah. A dancer from *Les Girls* was shot by a concreter and buried in the foundations of the Victoria Street apartments.

WILL: Fuck.

SHANE: Must have been drugs… Did you hear that creaking?

WILL: Nup.

SHANE: Yeah, it's a fuckin' ghost. If I see it I'm fuckin' leaving. I might do judo.

WILL: To take on a ghost?

SHANE: No, for self-defence. Get lessons. My brother used to do it. He was pretty good. He was in the paper heaps. And for swimming. He was good at stuff like that.

WILL: Right. Cool.

> *Slight pause.*

So…

SHANE: Yeah?

WILL: How's the bottlo?

SHANE: Oh, good. You haven't come in as much as when I first met you.

WILL: Nup.

SHANE: I was a mong when I served you, hey.

WILL: No.

SHANE: Yeah, I stuffed it all up and they couldn't balance the till. They took me off register for a while. I'm back on it now.

WILL: So what else have you been up to?

SHANE: Nothing. Just hanging out. I see this friend, this old friend. We have dinner sometimes.

WILL: Cool.

SHANE: Are those bits in your hair fake?

WILL: The blonder bits are highlights.

SHANE: Awesome. Do you use gel?

WILL: Wax.

SHANE: I use gel but it goes too hard. See?

WILL: Yeah. It's really hard.

SHANE: I was trying to cover up the chunky bits from when the hairdresser got the noddies. But this hair gel's too full-on and it gave me a headache from the spiky bits when I sleep. It's fully like glue and shit.

WILL: Yeah, get a better one.

SHANE: Yeah. Can I feel your wax?

WILL: Um. Yeah.

SHANE: Cool. Sticky. Your hair's nice.

WILL: Thanks.

SHANE: You smell good too.

WILL: It's Issey Miyake.

SHANE: Cool.

> SHANE *leans in to kiss* WILL. WILL *pulls away.*

WILL: So when will you start judo?

SHANE: I don't know. I only just thought of it.

WILL: [*karate-chopping* SHANE] Hee-ya.

SHANE: Piss off.

WILL: 'Abu-Kick'. Remember that? From *Mortal Kombat.*

SHANE: No, *Street Fighter II.*

WILL: Oh yeah.

SHANE: And it was 'Ryu-Ken'.

WILL: Was it? [*Playfully pushing* SHANE] 'Ryu-Ken'.

> *They begin to wrestle and at some point they roll about on top of each other.*

It wasn't 'Ryu-Ken'.

SHANE: Yes. Ryu and Ken were the ones who could use that move. You should do it with me.

WILL: Um. What?

SHANE: Judo.

WILL: Oh no. I don't need to.

SHANE: [*tough*] Oh yeah?

> *They continue to playfight.*

WILL: You're dead, fucker.

SHANE: [*tougher*] Oh yeah?

> WILL *squeezes a pressure point on* SHANE.

Ow.

WILL: Oh, diddums.

> WILL *squeezes a pressure point on* SHANE.

SHANE: Ow.

WILL: Pressure point.

> WILL *squeezes a pressure point on* SHANE.

SHANE: Ow.

WILL: Another one.

WILL *squeezes a pressure point on* SHANE.

SHANE: Ow.

WILL: Pressure point. Ha ha.

SHANE *pinches* WILL.

Ow, don't pinch, girl. Pressure point.

WILL *squeezes a pressure point on* SHANE.

SHANE: Ow. [*Slapping* WILL] Horsy-bite.

WILL: Don't spank, perv.

SHANE: How do you know where my pressure points are? My brother used to always do that. And this. [*Twisting* WILL's *nipple*] Now whistle. Whistle.

WILL *whistles.*

WILL: What?

SHANE: No, it's meant to hurt so much that you can't whistle.

WILL: I like it but.

SHANE: Oh well, you wouldn't if my brother did it.

WILL: I might.

SHANE: Yuck. No, he's gross. What about dribble torture?

WILL: What's that?

SHANE: Oh, it's fucked. He would hold me down like this.

SHANE *pins* WILL *down.* WILL *lets him.*

WILL: Yeah?

SHANE: And then let spit dribble down and suck it up just before it hit my face… if I was lucky.

WILL: Yuck.

SHANE: Festy, hey.

SHANE *looks as though he might spit.*

WILL: Don't do it.

SHANE: I won't. I'll just kiss you.

WILL: Okay.

They pash heaps. They start feeling each other's bodies.

SHANE: We better, um. [*Coughs*] Sorry, frog in my throat. We better, um, go under the sheet if we're going to do this. People can see.

WILL: Oh.

SHANE *lifts the bedsheet over them, covering them completely Their kisses grow in passion. It is apparent that they are feeling each other up.*

SHANE: It's a really dumb belt, I'm sorry. It's fully cowboy, hey.

WILL: You do it.

SHANE: I really liked it when you said 'Sit on my cock' at your place that time.

WILL: Cool.

SHANE: I'd never heard that saying before: 'Sit on my cock.'

WILL: Yeah.

SHANE: Yeah. It made me really horny.

WILL: Good.

SHANE: Sorry I didn't.

WILL: What?

SHANE: Sorry I didn't sit on your cock.

WILL: It's okay. Kiss me.

> *They kiss.*

SHANE: That felt nice. I like kissing you.

WILL: Yeah.

> *They kiss again.*

SHANE: Do you like it when I touch you there?

WILL: Let's just wank.

SHANE: You touch my balls.

WILL: Just wank.

SHANE: I liked it when you sat on my cock. I mean, that kind of didn't work, but when we changed positions and it did... that was so good.

WILL: Mmmm.

SHANE: One time you should root me. Do you like it?

WILL: Uh-ah.

> WILL *interrupts* SHANE *with a pash.*

SHANE: Oh, you're such a good pasher. Do you want me to fuck you again?

WILL: No.

SHANE: Okay. Why won't you touch me more?

> WILL *interrupts* SHANE *with a pash.*

Mmmh. I love…

WILL *interrupts* SHANE *with a pash.*

Ohh, do you want to cum soon?

WILL: Not yet.

SHANE: I love it when you just…

WILL *interrupts* SHANE *with a pash.*

Mmmh. I love it when you pash me suddenly like that.

WILL *interrupts* SHANE *with a pash.*

You're such a good kisser. My ex-best friend stayed at my house once and we woke up kissing in the middle of the night. It was so good.

WILL: Don't talk now.

SHANE: Cool. It's just you kiss like him…

WILL *interrupts* SHANE *with a pash.*

You're going to make me blow if you keep kissing me. I like your dick. I am going to blow soon. Do you want to blow?

WILL: Soon.

SHANE: Really soon?

WILL: No, wait.

SHANE: I don't think I can.

WILL: Not yet.

SHANE: I'm trying.

WILL: Soon.

SHANE: Let's blow together.

WILL: Okay.

SHANE: Now?

WILL: Soon.

SHANE: Make yourself blow.

WILL: Okay.

SHANE: Okay?

WILL: Not yet.

SHANE: Now?

WILL: Soon. Soon.

SHANE: Better go now. 'Cause I can't wait now.

WILL: Okay.

SHANE: Yes?

WILL: Yes.

SHANE: Oh. Hang on. Yes?

WILL: Yes.

SHANE: Now!

WILL: Yes. Yes! Yes! Yes?

SHANE: I went. Far out, mine shot so far. Did you see it?

WILL: Kind of.

> *They take the sheet off.*

SHANE: Mmh. I better take this to the laundromat.

WILL: [*sighing*] Fuck. It is a bit echoey in here.

> WILL *washes his hands in* SHANE'*s sink.*

SHANE: It's haunted. It's fucked. Sometimes it's fun to do it quick like that. We'll do it for longer next time but.

WILL: Yeah, no, it was good. I liked it.

SHANE: Me too. Even though we just wanked. Hey, you know how I don't have bum sex?

WILL: Yeah.

SHANE: It's not because I'm a virgin. I mean, I've got off with a boy, boys before, heaps and girls. I just haven't been fucked.

WILL: Oh no, that's fine. Don't worry about those things, Shane.

SHANE: Yeah. I had a boyfriend in Goulburn.

WILL: Cool.

SHANE: Yeah. Actually, he wasn't a boyfriend. He was my friend Joel.

WILL: Cool.

SHANE: Yeah but he's so immature.

WILL: Yeah, my ex sucks too.

SHANE: I bet you've had heaps of boyfriends.

WILL: Nah. Just one really.

SHANE: No way. You deserve more.

WILL: You're sweet.

SHANE: Sweet? You think I'm really young, hey.

WILL: No I don't.

SHANE: I'm nineteen. I just look young.

WILL: You're cute.

SHANE: Oh, you think I'm so little and young.

WILL: I don't.

SHANE: You do so.

WILL: I think you're hot.

SHANE: I can't wait to fuck you again. That was so good. At your place. In the shower. I can do it for longer when we fuck.

WILL: Oh well, next time.

SHANE: So there'll be a next time?

WILL: Maybe. Why not?

SHANE: I haven't seen you for a while.

WILL: Yeah. I'm sorry about that.

SHANE: Were you avoiding me?

WILL: No.

SHANE: Sure?

WILL: Yeah.

SHANE: Cool. I hope not.

SHANE *handles himself.*

Sorry, just readjusting.

WILL: What?

SHANE: My balls.

WILL: Are they uncomfortable?

SHANE: I don't know.

WILL: Maybe I was kind of avoiding you but…

SHANE: Why?

WILL: … I have a good reason.

SHANE: I'm really needy, hey.

WILL: No. No. Nothing about you. Look, Shane, I think I could have given you something.

SHANE: What?

WILL: It's like warts.

SHANE: Warts?

WILL: It's a papilloma virus.

SHANE: Oh my God, what is it?

WILL: No, don't worry. Look, it's just this thing I have. I had. Not this time. Last time. I'm cured now. This is embarrassing. It's just this thing that grows like a rash and it can make you sick at first but it's basically just a…

SHANE: We used a condom, I can't catch AIDS, I hope you know.

WILL: No. It's nothing like that. It's really common.

SHANE: How did I get it? We used a condom.

WILL: Don't worry, man. It's easy enough to treat.

SHANE: What is it?
WILL: It's warts. It's like warts. I had it on my arse.
SHANE: Yuck.
WILL: Thanks.
SHANE: Yuck.
WILL: I didn't know I had it when we met. Anyway, the doctor was pretty relaxed about it. I think you have it on your balls. I have a brochure for you and a letter from the specialist to take to your GP.

WILL *pulls out the brochure and note.*

SHANE: My GP's in Goulburn.
WILL: Just go to one here. Just take the note in.
SHANE: I can't afford it.
WILL: Doctor's are on Medicare.
SHANE: I don't have a Medicare card.
WILL: Go and get one.
SHANE: Specialists aren't on Medicare.
WILL: You might not have to go to a specialist.
SHANE: I'll have to go back to Goulburn.
WILL: Just go soon. It's so so okay. It's just bad luck.
SHANE: Bad luck! Fuck you, giving me some fuckin' gay disease.
WILL: Shane. It's okay.
SHANE: No it's not. Dirty…
WILL: Shane, I'm sorry.
SHANE: Don't come near me, freak. You fuckin' freak.
WILL: Shane, come on. Don't be stupid.
SHANE: I'm not stupid. You're fucked. I got eighty for my UAI, you fuck… you pretty cock-sucking fuckin' slut. You're fuckin' disgusting. I can't fuckin' believe… Dirty fucking gay cunt.
WILL: Shane, calm down.
SHANE: No! Fuck you. Sydney's full of fucking…
WILL: I'm going.
SHANE: It's so fucking gross. Shit.

SHANE *cries.*

WILL: Hey, don't cry.
SHANE: Oh man…
WILL: Don't you have someone to talk to? A sister or something? Sisters are really good with this sort of stuff.

SHANE: I don't have one.

WILL: Your brother?

SHANE: This is so fucked for me.

WILL: It's really really nothing.

SHANE: It is for me. It so is for me.

WILL: Just go in to any GP. I'll just leave the note here.

   WILL *puts down the brochure and note.*

SHANE: Don't go, Will. Stay here tonight. I'm so excellent if you get to know me.

   WILL *exits. A figure passes behind* SHANE.

Who the fuck is that?

   SHANE *inspects the room. There is no one there.*

PETER'*s apartment in Elizabeth Bay. Several weeks later.*

PETER *has answered the door to* SHANE. SHANE *is carrying an envelope.*

PETER: Hello Shane. I wasn't expecting you until later. I've only just started marinating the meat.

SHANE: Oh yeah, I was just on my way to post a letter and thought I'd pop in to say hi. Glad you're here.

PETER: Are you okay? You've been crying.

SHANE: No I haven't.

PETER: You have. I can tell. Look at the red under your eyes.

SHANE: It's those itchy-ball trees near the station. They make me teary.

PETER: I hope everything's okay.

SHANE: Yeah.

PETER: Is it a love letter you're posting?

SHANE: No. Just to some people in Goulburn. You framed the terrine drawing.

   The terrine drawing is unseen on the fourth wall.

PETER: Yes.

SHANE: It looks just like it. All the little meaty bits. It's really good, Peter.

PETER: Yeah, I'm not that happy.

SHANE: It must have taken ages.

PETER: No, I just copied the photo out of the recipe book. Oh, the bloody cat still hasn't eaten its Whiskas.

SHANE: Is she missing again?

PETER: No, she finally came back but she's strange. I think she's found a tom. The slut. She was walking around here spraying her pheromones everywhere.

SHANE: What does she look like?

PETER: Just a mongrel tabby. I wish I could do that—just go into Stonewall and scent people.

SHANE: Yeah.

PETER: Can I get you a wine? I just opened some brie.

SHANE: Bree? My brother's girlfriend's called Bree. It's not her you're talking about but.

PETER: No, it's cheese.

SHANE: Nah, I'm right.

PETER: Is it that boy who made you cry?

SHANE: I haven't been crying.

PETER: You've been very hard to get out of the house lately.

SHANE: I was sick.

PETER: Lovesick, I bet.

SHANE: But I think it was just that seafood salad stuff that I like.

PETER: Don't eat that stuff. But there's something else. With the boy.

SHANE: He's a cock. We had a fight.

PETER: When?

SHANE: Few weeks ago. He finally got my messages. He came over and he's so fucked.

PETER: Did he break it off?

SHANE: I wasn't going out with him. It wasn't a boyfriend thing. As if.

PETER: Oh well. Move on.

SHANE: Yeah. And um, I was thinking, I might need you to take me to…

PETER: Stonewall? No worries, I'll just grab my scent.

SHANE: You're funny.

PETER: Funnier than Will?

SHANE: No.

PETER: I hate him. I bet he's gorgeous.

SHANE: Whatever. Well, he is actually kind of hot. He has those lines.

PETER: What lines?

SHANE: Those Van Damme lines that angle towards his, you know…

PETER: His lunch.

SHANE: I couldn't send the letter that I was going to post. It was to home.

PETER: Don't get embarrassed and change the subject. I've told you about a lot of my roots over dinner and a glass or two. It's about your turn.

SHANE: Okay. But this isn't going into your wank bank, is it?

PETER: Yes, a long-term deposit that'll earn a lot of interest.

SHANE: Don't be gross. I'll only tell you because you're my friend and that's what best friends do. They sit around talking about, well, girls and boys.

PETER: I know.

SHANE: Yeah. He has a really smooth stomach. A six-pack.

PETER: Oh shit. Wait, start from the top.

SHANE: No. That's all. He sucks. With his friggin' expensive girl's hair-do and…

PETER: What colour?

SHANE: It has blond highlight bits.

PETER: Very gay.

SHANE: Yeah, he's not like a pansy but. I wouldn't like that. I mean, his voice is a bit gay but not too gay.

PETER: Not like mine.

SHANE: Yours isn't too gay.

PETER: Oh good.

SHANE: His is like a normal boy's but also a bit gay so that it reminds you that you can have sex with him.

PETER: Yours is like that.

SHANE: Mine isn't gay at all.

PETER: Oh, isn't it?

SHANE: No. Oh, and he so knows that his eyes are really good. He shows them off so much. Like just looks at you. He totally misled me.

PETER: Don't play dumb. It takes two to tango. What's his skin like?

SHANE: Oh, it's soft. Like expensive soft. 'Cause I think he's rich. Like just spends money on stuff. So he smells nice too.

PETER: Like what?

SHANE: Is-he-markie.
PETER: Does he smell like fucking?
SHANE: What?
PETER: Sorry.
SHANE: I don't know.
PETER: Go on.
SHANE: With what?
PETER: Is he strong?
SHANE: Stronger than me. He's tall. Heaps taller than me. He must be six foot. He could pin me down.
PETER: Heavens.
SHANE: When he came to my house, we wrestled.
PETER: Wrestled?
SHANE: Yeah. That was my favourite bit. I felt like Mum was going to bust us for jumping on the bed or something but I didn't know he was a filthy fuckwit then.
PETER: Have you seen him with his shirt off?
SHANE: Yeah. At his house.
PETER: I love shirts coming off. It's always been my favourite bit.
SHANE: My favourite thing about him are his shoulders. He's huge. He's like a footy player. When he took his shirt off—his shoulders are like balls of muscle. And I like his lips. The line where it stops being lips and starts being face or the other way round is really, I don't know, like I made it up. It's like it's drawn.
PETER: And are his lips kissable?
SHANE: Yeah. And he's good at tonguing.
PETER: Oh really?
SHANE: Yeah.
PETER: I can imagine the shirt coming off.
SHANE: He has a little bit of soft hair in like a 'V' here [*indicating his upper chest*]. I think he clippers it but it's grown a bit so now it's soft. And he has a pretty hard chest. His nipples are low and brown and that's how I like them.
PETER: Me too. What's his body hair like?
SHANE: Um, it's kind of light brown. His tan has no gaps.
PETER: None?
SHANE: Nup. And yeah, he's hot.
PETER: Keep on going.

SHANE: With what?

PETER: You want to tell me about his cock.

SHANE: Okay, well, it's good. When I slipped his undies down he had a half-mongrel. It was just starting to move to one side and then up.

PETER: Goodness.

SHANE: I watched it grow. It's pretty big. It's thick.

PETER: Are you hard now?

SHANE: Yeah. A bit. My brother caught me with a boy once.

PETER: What else? Tell me more. Did the mongrel get full-on?

SHANE: Are you?

PETER: What?

SHANE: Hard?

PETER: A bit. Are you more hard now?

SHANE: Yes. I want to be your friend.

PETER: Well, that's okay. Friends do this sort of thing all the time.

> SHANE *stands and undoes his belt.* PETER *gets on his knees. He starts to pull* SHANE*'s pants down.*

SHANE: My brother reckons faggots spread disease and they fuck kids and they're weak. Maybe that's true.

PETER: I'm sorry?

SHANE: I'm not like your other friends. I'm special.

PETER: All right, Shane. No is fine. But don't carry on with bullshit. You know what's going on. You can't play the little kid for ever.

SHANE: But I am a kid.

PETER: Stop. Just stop it. It shits me. It really shits me when people your age pretend. The little country kid who has no idea will only go so far. For fuck sake, switch on, Shane. Grow up and stop acting so fucking pathetic.

SHANE: I'm sixteen. I'm halfway through Year Ten.

PETER: But you said…

SHANE: I was lying.

PETER: Why?

SHANE: I ran away from home when my brother bashed the fuck out of me. You've done this before.

PETER: I beg your pardon.

SHANE: Yuck. Old sleaze.

PETER: Maybe you should go.

SHANE: You make me sick, ye dirty perv.
PETER: You're frightening me.
SHANE: Ye fuckin' cunt.
PETER: Just go, please. Get out.

♦ ♦ ♦ ♦ ♦

SHANE *is now in the laundromat, doing his washing.*

He has a pile of linen and coins for the machine. He takes his laundry liquid out of his sports bag.

BEN *enters. He is carrying the same envelope that* SHANE *held in the previous scene.*

BEN: How are ya, little bro?

END OF ACT ONE

Brett Stiller as Ben in the Griffin Theatre Company production of STRANGERS
IN BETWEEN, 2005. (Photo: Robert McFarlane)

ACT TWO

The laundromat. Continuing from the previous scene.

SHANE: Fuck. Don't come near me, Ben.

BEN: Fuckin' hell. I've driven halfway across the country, putting up signs and looking for you, Shane. Some cunt said you were in Byron. Mum and Dad are in fuckin' Mildura 'cause someone said you were picking fuckin' fruit and here you are in a fuckin' laundromat.

SHANE: Why did you come?

BEN: Because I wanted to find you. I've taken heaps of time off work.

SHANE: Don't come any closer.

BEN: This letter turned up.

SHANE: Beg ye' pardon?

BEN: Been looking everywhere for you. Then the letter turned up.

SHANE: I never posted it.

BEN: It had a postmark on it so you must have.

SHANE: No I never. It's still up in my room.

BEN: It said Kings Cross post office.

SHANE: I don't think there is a Kings Cross post office.

BEN: There is.

SHANE: Is not. Don't come near me, Ben.

BEN: The bloke at the bottle shop said you'd be here. Cool place to work. Cases were expensive but. Posher than I thought around here.

SHANE: Are you drunk?

BEN: Too expensive.

SHANE: Toohey's Red's not expensive.

BEN: It's mid-strength.

SHANE: Toohey's Red's not mid-strength.

BEN: Yes it is.

SHANE: It's just on special.

BEN: Whatever. It's mid-strength.

SHANE: Whatever. It's not. I work there. I'd know.

BEN: Well, it is. You're wrong.

SHANE: You have to go.

BEN: So what's wrong with you? You sick?

SHANE: How'd you know that?

BEN: You are sick. Contagious?

SHANE: No. I'm not sick.

BEN: Said in your letter. What'd you need the Medicare number for?

SHANE: I don't. You're making it up.

BEN: Well, you can just get your own Medicare number so you fucked that up.

SHANE: I'm fine. There's nothing wrong with me.

BEN: Even Rocky misses you, hey.

SHANE: The fuckin' dog does not miss me.

BEN: She does. She's getting heaps fat now. Dad feeds her. He's been giving her two-minute noodles every night and Woollies' chickens on the weekends if they're reduced. Mum's stopped stopping him. It's comfort food because Rocky's missing you so much.

SHANE: Well, I don't believe that. I miss Rocky but. Did Dad want you to find me?

BEN: Yes.

SHANE: I bet Mum made youse.

BEN: No.

SHANE: I can tell you're lying. You and Dad hate me.

BEN: Shane, don't be a dick.

SHANE: Yeah, that's right. Criticise me all the time why don't ya?

BEN: Don't be over-sensitive.

SHANE: Over-sensitive. Whatever, cockhead.

BEN: Shane, come on. Do you wanna go to Maccas and have a chat?

SHANE: To the café bit?

BEN: If you want?

SHANE: No. You wouldn't just come in here. You can't just come in here and pretend everything's okay, Ben.

BEN: You know practically the whole town's been trying to find you?

SHANE: Do they know what you did to me?

BEN: I don't know.

SHANE: Things get around. They should know.

BEN: Well…

SHANE: Fuckin' psycho. It's not my problem. And anyway, I don't think you are my brother no more.

BEN: Mr Hewson died. He had a heart attack watching telly. The go-kart track might close now.

SHANE: I reckon I'm allowed to feel how I feel too. I don't reckon there's any reason for me to feel bad about what I've done. To anyone.

BEN: They reckon Tim Hewson might get a contract with Maserati which is fuckin' bullshit. Look at Martin Luke. He got into the Kangaroos and everything and now he's fat and hopeless... it's all just bullshit. Everything. Sad Tim's dad died first but, hey?

SHANE: I've wanted to say for ages that I reckon you're a psycho, Ben.

BEN: I got punched in the head outside Pashes last week

SHANE: That wasn't last week.

BEN: Still bruised.

SHANE: Goulburn's got worse. It's got meaner.

BEN: Nah, it was one of my mates.

SHANE: Who?

BEN: Box-head done it. He was pissed but and we're mates again now. See, that's what blokes do. They forgive and...

SHANE: No, fuck off. Don't tell me what to do.

BEN: Shane, I'm going through a hard time, you know that. Think about stuff. And I broke up with Bree.

SHANE: When? Again?

BEN: I've been seeing this girl Tarrine.

SHANE: I didn't know that. I went to school with her. She left Goulburn.

BEN: No, she's back.

SHANE: She's too young for you.

BEN: Yeah, I know. And she's a slut. I kind of hate her but I don't know. I just let things get to me sometimes and...

SHANE: Because you smoked too much pot.

BEN: No I don't.

SHANE: You had a billy everyday for breakfast.

BEN: No, Shane, don't say shit about stuff you don't know about. Who said I had a billy for breakfast everyday?

SHANE: You did. You told me that.

BEN: Pot just makes you forgetful. It doesn't do anything bad.

SHANE: It made you mean.

BEN: No it didn't. I don't smoke everyday anyway. I don't smoke that much at all. You're full of shit, you are.

SHANE: Well, something made you into a psycho.

BEN: No it didn't.

SHANE: Yes it did. I used to want to be like you when I grew up.

BEN: Err, whatever, fuck ya.

SHANE: I said not to come near me, Ben.

BEN: Are you going to come back home?

SHANE: No.

BEN: I got my hair cut. Do you like it?

SHANE: Kind of. I heard about Goulburn a few weeks back. About Reg.

BEN: Yeah, well…

SHANE: Are Mum and Dad still friends with him?

BEN: Yeah.

SHANE: But is he going to prison?

BEN: No. Newspaper's full of shit. I reckon we should go and get an ice block or something. It's hot. We could try to find Sunny Boys. Remember them?

SHANE: Nup.

BEN: Err, fuckin' dumb. Yes you do.

SHANE: No I don't.

BEN: Like a frozen popper. You do.

SHANE: I can't remember them.

BEN: Yes, you loved them. Sunny Boys.

SHANE: Maybe. They come in purple and orange?

BEN: Yeah, your favourite.

SHANE: I think I remember them. They weren't my favourite.

BEN: Yes they were. Let's go find them. I was thinking about them the other day.

SHANE: I don't think they make them any more.

BEN: They would.

SHANE: You reckon?

BEN: Yep, definitely.

SHANE: Well, I can't leave here and I don't want an iceblock.

BEN: Why not?

SHANE: I'm waiting for my washing to finish and I've got stuff soaking in NapiSan.

BEN: I'll wait.

SHANE: No. I need to wash my stuff a few times and the water needs to be boiling, and it takes ages. So no.

BEN: Well, whatever. It is fuckin' hot.

SHANE: I've been listening to the news heaps. Is it true what Angela Bresnik is saying about what happened at the pool?

BEN: She's lying. She just wants to be on *A Current Affair*. Reg trained me the most. That's why I'm the one who knows it couldn't be true. It's so dumb when newspapers say stuff like that. When I was a kid they said I was going to swim at the Olympics. Just because the newspaper says something. It actually means shit. Goulburn's shit. And now everyday it's about kiddy fiddlers.

SHANE: And it's like—remember teachers going on about 'Stranger Danger'? That fucked me up. Remember the picture on the stickers of that freaky dude with the evil eyes and the black coat? That was so fucked.

BEN: I've almost got my drainage apprenticeship.

SHANE: I know that. That was before.

BEN: Yeah. Only a few months to go.

SHANE: Then what?

BEN: I'll probably get heaps of work.

SHANE: That's good.

BEN: I'll get heaps of money. I could probably start my own business.

SHANE: How?

BEN: Get a loan. Interest rates are low. And just flog my boss's clients. He's a lazy rude fuck anyway so it wouldn't be wrong to take people away from him.

SHANE: That sounds good then.

BEN: I wanna get a new car too.

SHANE: Sell yours?

BEN: Yeah. Might sell it up here. Probably get more up here. Thought I might get you to help me. Where are you staying up here?

SHANE: I got a good place. I like it. I'm doing okay. It's got a yard and everything.

BEN: Where is it?

SHANE: I'm not going to tell you, Ben.

BEN: Why not?

SHANE: I don't want you around me any more.

BEN: Well… No one would hurt you back in Goulburn, Shane. I'd protect you, hey.

SHANE: What if I need protecting from you?

BEN: You reckon you're safe now?

SHANE: Hey?

BEN: Around here. A lot of weirdos.

SHANE: Oh, nah...

BEN: Shane, fuck, people are fucked up around here. There's like boy prostitutes and everything. That wall thing. Under the Coke sign.

SHANE: It's not under the Coke sign. It's the wall of the old gaol.

BEN: Oh, you know it, do you?

SHANE: No.

BEN: People might fuck you up, Shane. A homeless guy got scalped by vigilantes from Sutherland that want all the homeless people off the streets.

SHANE: I sleep with the radio on for security so I hear all the news. It seems dodgy around here but I've never had any trouble.

BEN: Well, still...

SHANE: I'm staying here.

BEN: How will you get by?

SHANE: I am getting by so that's okay, hey. Just let me finish my washing.

BEN: All right. So, I should go then. Goodbye Shane.

    BEN *moves closer to* SHANE, *perhaps to hug him.*

SHANE: Don't touch me. Fuck off.

BEN: You've got to look after yourself. You're just little and young.

SHANE: I'll call the police.

BEN: They're targeting seat belts; I saw a sign.

SHANE: Just keep away.

BEN: I'll tell Mum and Dad you're okay.

SHANE: No. Just tell them I don't want anyone to come near me and I'm moving on anyway. They won't be able to find me.

BEN: Okay. Should we shake hands at least?

    They shake hands. BEN *doesn't let go.*

SHANE: See ya.

BEN: Shane... You could come back, you know?

SHANE: Let go of my hand.

BEN: Shane, come back.

SHANE: Let go of my hand.

BEN: You're excellent, Shane.

SHANE: Let go of my fuckin' hand, Ben.
BEN: I want to get to know you again.
SHANE: I said let go, cunt.

> *Whack!* SHANE *hits* BEN *with the child-size cricket bat that he keeps in his laundry bag.*

I warned you. I warned you, Ben. Get out. I don't exist any more. Pretend you couldn't find me. I mean it. I never want to see you again.

> BEN *stumbles back. His ear is pounding. The blow has sent him into a daze. He almost falls backwards, shaking his head in disbelief.*

◆ ◆ ◆ ◆ ◆

Instantly we are on the landing in front of WILL's *door. A month or two later.*

WILL *has emerged, shaking his head in disbelief.*

SHANE: Hi Will. It's me, Shane. You haven't forgotten me, have ya?
WILL: Just surprised to see you. What do you want?
SHANE: How are you going?
WILL: Good. What d'ye want?
SHANE: So… Um… I was going to go play cricket. Can't play it on the road here. Play it in the park but. Wanna come? Cool shoes.
WILL: Look, I'm busy. I've got people inside.
SHANE: I got sacked from my job yesterday.
WILL: That's bad luck.
SHANE: Yeah. They're cunts.
WILL: I'm so not in the mood for this. Sorry.
SHANE: Tired?
WILL: Um… I've got family over and…
SHANE: Do you want me to come back later?
WILL: Not really.
SHANE: I can tell you want to get back inside.
WILL: That's right.
SHANE: How many brothers and sisters have you got?
WILL: Um… Two of each.

SHANE: Cool. Do they live nearby?

WILL: Yeah. One's moving. It's a goodbye lunch. I have to go.

SHANE: Was there a falling out?

WILL: No. She's just buying a house. Interest rates are low or something.

SHANE: Are your parents here too?

WILL: Um yeah. It's a family thing.

SHANE: I reckon your Mum and Dad would be cool.

WILL: Shane, I don't need this. And I'm coming down so it's not good timing.

SHANE: What do you mean, 'coming down'?

WILL: I took a pill last night so I'm feeling down.

SHANE: What kind of pill?

WILL: Ecstasy.

SHANE: Drugs?

WILL: Yeah.

SHANE: Why would you take something that makes you feel down?

WILL: It makes you feel good first.

SHANE: Keep your fluids up. Not too much but. That's how Katie Bender died.

WILL: Who?

SHANE: Oh no, she died when the Canberra Hospital exploded.

WILL: Right.

SHANE: They were demolishing it. Even people from Goulburn went to see it. It was meant to implode.

WILL: So, um… I better go back inside. I'm watching *The Wiggles* with my nephew.

SHANE: They're creepy, hey.

WILL: Yeah. I like them today. Bye.

SHANE: I just came back because you make me horny.

> WILL *scoffs.*

I wank about us.

WILL: I'm touched.

SHANE: You know how good your eyes are. I know you know. Do you want a head job?

WILL: Fuckin' hell. I'm fine, thanks.

SHANE: Like later. I could come back.

WILL: No thanks.

SHANE: I can tell you're a bit turned on by that.

WILL: No.

SHANE: Can I tell you something?

WILL: I've gotta go back inside.

SHANE: My favourite thing about you is your lips. They're so good. I reckon they look drawn on. I'll go. Can I just have one more kiss? Just one more kiss. I won't bother you any more. Cross my heart. Please.

Maybe WILL *considers it.*

WILL: I'm going.

SHANE: I'd love to meet your family.

WILL: Another time.

SHANE: Really?

WILL: Um. No.

SHANE: I wouldn't embarrass you in front of them. They wouldn't think I'm gay.

WILL: They wouldn't care about that.

SHANE: Do you introduce boys to them?

WILL: I could. But, um, there's nothing really between us, anyway, so…

SHANE: You wouldn't know anyone who could give me a job, would ya?

WILL: Nup.

SHANE: I'm going to get evicted if I don't pay my rent soon.

WILL: You're not having a good time.

SHANE: Do you know how to get on the dole? I could get it, hey.

WILL: Yeah. Guess so.

SHANE: It's Centrelink, hey.

WILL: Yeah.

SHANE: Would I need papers and stuff?

WILL: They'll be able to tell you.

SHANE: I couldn't use your phone, could I?

WILL: Couldn't you just use a public phone?

SHANE: Yeah. Sure. So um… you did give me those warts.

WILL: Sorry.

SHANE: They got really bad.

WILL: Sorry.

SHANE: Which doctor did you go to? I want a good one.

WILL: Haven't you been yet?

SHANE: Not yet. Do you have another one of those letters? I threw it out.

WILL: You probably should go pretty soon.

SHANE: Yeah. You're telling me. They've got pretty bad.

WILL: How bad?

SHANE: Infected, I think. Festy. Colourful.

WILL: Fuckin' hell. Shit. You gotta look after yourself, dude.

SHANE: I was scared to go in by myself.

WILL: Why?

SHANE: Could you come in with me?

WILL: I don't think I need to.

SHANE: Do you know that I'm younger than you think?

WILL: What do you mean?

SHANE: I'm in Year Ten.

WILL: Fuck. Where?

SHANE: Nowhere now.

WILL: Right.

SHANE: I'm sixteen so…

WILL: Well, Shane, Um… Call me, if… I mean, I don't know what I can do for you.

SHANE: I know were not going to…

WILL: Yeah, we're not. Don't put any expectations on me but… If you really need someone to… I don't know. Just look after yourself. Go see a doctor. Today.

SHANE: Yeah.

WILL: Promise?

SHANE: Yeah.

WILL: And um…

WILL *reaches into his wallet and pulls out a fifty-dollar note.*

You've got other friends. Don't you?

SHANE: Yep. Another friend.

WILL: Good.

WILL *gives* SHANE *a peck on the cheek.*

Take this too.

WILL *hands* SHANE *the money.*

SHANE: Oh, ye sure?

WILL: Yeah. It's fine.

SHANE: Thanks, mate.

WILL: See ya.

> *They shake hands.*

SHANE: You're excellent, WILL.

> SHANE *releases* WILL*'s hand.*

WILL: Bye.

> WILL *exits.*

♦ ♦ ♦ ♦ ♦

PETER*'s door. Some days later.*

PETER *is wearing a rather feminine kitchen apron.*

PETER: Mmm. What have we got here?

SHANE: I was just nearby and thought I'd knock.

PETER: Did you?

SHANE: Thought I'd say g'day. See how you're going.

PETER: Fine.

SHANE: That's good. I was hoping I'd just run into you but I'm not working at the bottlo any more.

PETER: You puzzle me, Shane.

SHANE: Can I come in?

PETER: Shane, some things were said…

SHANE: Sometimes mates fight.

PETER: What do you want, Shane?

SHANE: Just thought I'd see how you are. Did your cat come back?

PETER: No. They go away to die.

SHANE: Poor cat.

PETER: Yes but death seemed to make her very horny.

SHANE: Did you cry?

PETER: Just a cat. I'm not some lonely old poof with a cat, am I?

SHANE: No.

PETER: No. I've got my pot plants now.

SHANE: Oh, good.

PETER: It was good to catch up with you, Shane.

SHANE: Oh. Do you wanna go have a coffee or something?

PETER: Bit busy actually. And look, Shane. I don't like it when you claim, like Graeme claims, like everyone thinks, that just because an older man takes an interest that he's thinking with his dick. It wasn't like that. I enjoyed your company. That's all.

SHANE: I'm weird. I've gone weird, Peter. I talk to myself. I've gone fucked in the head. I don't know what I'm saying sometimes.

PETER: Was it true? What you told me?

SHANE: What?

PETER: About you? About your brother?

SHANE: Yes. Promise it is. They couldn't get him off me. It was bad. He broke the bit of bone in my cheek that's like a tabletop. It was completely crushed. He was like a bull terrier. He even growled. It was so fucked. I'm not making it up. I just can't work out why he went psycho.

PETER: You must hate him.

SHANE: No. No I don't. I've been trying to pluck up the courage to go home but I can't. There's no way I can go back and I… I have to go to hospital, hey.

PETER: What for?

SHANE: It doesn't matter.

PETER: What? It does matter. Tell me.

SHANE: I have an STD.

PETER: What is it?

SHANE: It's a bad one.

PETER: Oh… What?

SHANE: Warts.

PETER: Warts! Oh no, that's fine. Bit of nitrogen or whatever. They freeze them off. Watch them though because you can have a recurrence. I had them once and it took five goes to get rid of them. Either that or I had warty trade five nights in a row and one mustn't discount that possibility.

SHANE: Mine's past that. It's on my arse and my balls. All across my Mars bar. I left it.

PETER: What's a Mars bar?

SHANE: It's the bridge bit from your balls to your arse.

PETER: Oh. I'm going to use that.

SHANE: I should have gone to the doctor. I just couldn't work out how. At home I would have just asked my mum to take me. But anyway, I went and it was awful. The doctor said, 'Why didn't you come to see me earlier? Were you hoping to grow a beanbag on your arse?'

PETER: What a hoot.

SHANE: And I just cried. I don't want to be a freak. I didn't know they would get this bad. I thought they would just go away.

PETER: You could have come and told me that. I used to get STDs all the time. I remember my first one. I thought Satan was forcing himself out of my penis. I was a Christian then. Don't ask. But I found out I had the clap and they just give you a jab and it goes. Of course, some things aren't that easy to get rid of and, of course, they're all serious.

SHANE: I wore a condom.

PETER: Yes, you can still get stuff though. They say to even wear a condom for head now but, I mean, really, you might as well stay at home and suck on a dildo.

SHANE: Yeah, well, I haven't had sex for ages.

PETER: Oh, you poor thing. Join the club. I'm on the ladies' auxiliary. So what happens now?

SHANE: I have to go to hospital they're so bad.

PETER: When do you go in?

SHANE: I'm waiting for a place. It'll be day surgery.

PETER: Oh well, that'll be fine.

SHANE: They put me out and everything.

PETER: Yes, they'll give you lovely drugs.

SHANE: Yeah. Well, I have to have someone to collect me. They said I have to have someone.

PETER: I'll do it.

SHANE: Will you? It might be a weekday.

PETER: I'll take the day off.

SHANE: I'll pay for the cab.

PETER: No you won't.

SHANE: You won't have to take the whole day off. You just need to be there to 'escort me home' in case I'm too spasticated from the drugs.

PETER: I'll take the day off and I'll sit and wait for you. We'll go together in the morning. It will be 'awesome'.

SHANE: I'll wake up as soon as I can.

PETER: It'll be fine, Shane.

SHANE: I know you said you hate hospitals because of your mum.

PETER: Did I say that?

SHANE: Yeah, you hate the smell.

PETER: Oh well, no but that's true enough. But this sounds like the perfect excuse for the day off work.

SHANE: I didn't have anyone to ask. When they said I had to have someone I said, 'What if I have no one?' and they said I must have someone.

PETER: And they were right.

SHANE: I don't like hospitals.

PETER: Have your family contacted you?

SHANE: Not a peep. They don't care and I can't go back.

PETER: Are you hungry? I could make you something. A piece of sticky date pudding?

SHANE: Okay.

PETER: It was a joke.

SHANE: Oh. Shut up.

PETER: Come in. Make yourself comfortable. Wish I had a beanbag to offer you.

SHANE: I said shut up.

> PETER *exits.*

◆ ◆ ◆ ◆ ◆

SHANE*'s place. Some weeks later.*

SHANE *takes out a half-packed travel bag and some stuff to make a sandwich. His arse is itchy.*

BEN *enters.*

SHANE: Fuck. No way. Please don't hurt me, Ben. I'm sorry.

BEN: I'm not here for trouble. I thought we could go for a swim. Have you got togs?

SHANE: How'd you… My door was locked.

BEN: It wasn't.

SHANE: It always is.

SHANE *retrieves his cricket bat from his bed.*

BEN: You can hit me again if you want.

SHANE: I might.

BEN: If it makes you feel better.

SHANE: You've gone weird. Who told you I lived here? Those bottleshop cunts. I didn't take any money. They're fucked. Did they see one of your signs? I've never seen one. I've been looking for them. Where do you put them up?

BEN: I need to talk. I just need to talk. Please. I'm your brother. Can't you trust me? I promise I won't hurt you. Put the bat down, mate.

SHANE: No. Why can't you disappear out of my life?

BEN: I've tried. But it won't work. Come back. Mum's waiting for you to come back. You should see her hair but. She came home from the hairdresser and it was so big and curly. It was like she'd gone in and asked to look like Barnsie in Chisel. Fuck, Dad and me laughed. Couldn't help it. I was ripped so I couldn't stop. Mum cried and I got paranoid but then she laughed and it was okay. We don't laugh much no more. She can't sleep. She has nightmares. Tim Hewson looks like he will get a contract with Maserati. The paper was right for once. After his dad's funeral he was straight on a plane to Europe. They'll pay him heaps. His dad was watching car racing when he died. People die all the time in Goulburn. That's all old people talk about, hey. A pipe bust open on me the other day. Shit poured on me and everything. Everyone laughed. I didn't snap. I'm not going to get into fights no more. There's heaps of Lebs in Goulburn. They're moving there from Sydney. It's dangerous. They fight in packs. If one gets you on the ground, ten cousins'll jump out of Holdens and kick the shit out of you. They live in the hills and prowl at night. A baby got taken from the hospital. It was hot as all fuck on the road. Was worried my new tyres would melt. Nan might not move down the coast no more. There are Lebs there too. And junkies. Junkie Lebs. Terrorist junkie Lebs everywhere and the drought. Council's got to do something. More roundabouts. Ivan Milat's running for alderman but. Shooters Party and a Family First preference deal, they reckon. It's such a hot day. Come back. We'd drive straight to the pool. Straight down the highway. Straight through town. Straight to the pool. Dive in and swim to the other side.

SHANE: You just want to beat me in a race.

BEN: I'd let you win.

SHANE: Are Mum's nightmares about me?

BEN: You could come back because it's not your fault.

SHANE: You're not yourself.

BEN: I hurt you. I remembered your face. I remembered seeing your face. I saw it in my sleep. All the time. I reckon you see it in yours.

SHANE: I'm scared of you.

BEN: You looked so shocked. I don't know what made you look like that. I hurt you. But I don't think it was my fault. I wasn't me. It wasn't me hurting you. I was someone else. It wasn't anything to do with you. I hate them. I hate them so much.

SHANE: Who?

BEN: I don't want you to be one of them. They hurt me too.

SHANE: Ben, I've never seen you like this.

BEN: I've always been like this inside.

SHANE: Why?

BEN: I'm sad.

SHANE: Ben, are you okay?

BEN: I miss you, Shane. Don't move further away.

SHANE: Some things can't be undone, Ben.

BEN: Maybe I want to hurt myself, Shane, not you.

SHANE: Why?

BEN: I want you to be the one to find my letter.

SHANE: Don't do that.

BEN: Then come back. It's such a hot day. I haven't been to the pool for ages.

SHANE: Are you okay now, Ben?

BEN: I don't know. I feel strange.

SHANE: It's like you're coming down.

BEN: I'm not a druggo, Shane. You think I am.

SHANE: No I don't. Maybe I can make you a sandwich. I'm making a sandwich to give to my friend. I have really nice bread and stuff. I was going to make him a really full-on one. I could make you one too.

BEN: What's going on, Shane?

SHANE: Come and help me make a sandwich. Would you like that?

BEN: Yeah.

SHANE: I've got chicken luncheon. You like that, hey.

BEN: Chicken loaf?

SHANE: Chicken loaf. I knew there was another name for it. It says 'chicken luncheon' on the packet. I knew we called it something different. I couldn't remember. Chicken loaf.

BEN: 'Pressed chicken.' Some people say that. Not us but.

SHANE: I have devon too.

BEN: I hate that.

SHANE: I love it. I got this kind of lettuce. It's called 'rocket' which is cool.

BEN: Yeah, I've had that. It's spicy lettuce.

SHANE: Is it?

BEN: Yeah.

> SHANE *makes two sandwiches as he talks.*

SHANE: Cool. I got mustard. I spent heaps. But I wanted it to be a good sandwich.

BEN: Yeah. I should bring you up some of Mum's relish.

SHANE: Nah, I've always hated Mum's relish.

BEN: No, Shane, it's an acquired taste. That's what she says and she's right.

SHANE: Maybe.

BEN: It's true.

SHANE: I have cordial as well. Do you like fruit-cup cordial?

BEN: I love it. You know that.

SHANE: Okay then.

> SHANE *prepares a cup of cordial for* BEN.

BEN: Fuck, it's a hot day. Wish I could just go for a swim.

SHANE: I'm going to make the cordial really strong.

BEN: Good.

> *Pause.*

Remember how Reg used to say there was a chemical that would make your wee go fluoro pink?

SHANE: Yeah.

BEN: I believed that. I still haven't ever pissed in a pool since. Funny, hey. I guess there could be a chemical for that but it probably is bullshit, hey.

SHANE: Yeah. I always thought Reg was a mean cunt.

BEN: Yeah. I think maybe he was. I used to love the pool but. Remember we used to kick up such a fuckin' stink when we'd wake up so early

on a Saturday and have to go and Dad'd threaten us with the strap.
You'd hate getting in but once you were, you wouldn't want to get
out. I loved the pool. Do you reckon someone would have punched
Reg's head in in prison yet?

SHANE: Probably. Is he in Goulburn, is he?

BEN: Yeah. It's too close but. I agree with the paper. They should have
put him in another maximum security.

SHANE: Are you squares or triangles?

BEN: Squares.

SHANE: I'm triangles.

> SHANE *cuts the sandwiches and hands* BEN'*s over.*

BEN: Thanks, mate.

SHANE: I heard something about Reg's lawyer getting him isolated.

BEN: That's fucked but. That's the reason people go to prison. Otherwise
just put him in the Olympia Motel or something. Fuck him. He
wrecked people's lives. Strong cordial.

SHANE: Yeah. Do Joanne and Paul still live in town?

BEN: They had to move away.

SHANE: Poor cunts.

BEN: Yeah, poor cunts. He never touched his own kids but.

SHANE: Did he ever touch you?

> BEN *eats his sandwich in silence.* SHANE *doesn't touch his.*

BEN: Yes.

SHANE: Did I see?

BEN: No.

SHANE: You remembered seeing my face. I looked shocked. Was it
there? Was I little?

BEN: It's a hot day today.

SHANE: Where did you see my face?

BEN: I don't know where. I didn't know what was happening. We could
try to find Sunny Boys.

SHANE: What did I see?

BEN: I don't know. I don't know if he made you or if you were just
there. I hope he didn't make you. But it only happened one time of
heaps of times. You saw.

SHANE: Was it at the pool?

BEN: Me just standing there letting him because I was his best swimmer.
You saw. You saw all that. You must have forgotten.

SHANE: That's what was happening.

BEN: It's true. You saw. You saw me with a stiffy too. He used to give me a stiffy. And you saw. Is that what made you into a 'you-know'?

SHANE: No. That's not... No one could think that.

BEN: They could. You saw. You left. Mum and Dad couldn't protect me either. As if I'd cry, Shane. You're just making that up. I never cry.

BEN *wipes away a tear.*

You can't go back because I'll beat the fuck out of you. No one will be able to stop me.

SHANE: You can't hurt me any more, Ben.

BEN: When I saw you with that little kid in your room. You're fuckin' disgusting. I can't fuckin' believe...

SHANE: Little kid? That was Joel. He's fifteen.

BEN: Don't come near me, freak. You fuckin' freak.

SHANE: He's not a little kid. He just looks young.

BEN: He's hasn't developed yet. You're like Reg.

SHANE: Is that what you think? He's fifteen. You know that. He was in my class. It's not like I'm old. You just don't get it. You're scared. You can't be scared of us: we weren't hurting anyone. We were just... I loved Joel. And I... I don't want you to hurt yourself.

BEN *eats in silence.*

I wish you would come to the Cross and put up signs.

BEN *finishes his sandwich and picks some crumbs off the plate.*

I don't have anyone. No one knows me here, Ben. I'm really alone. Come find me.

PETER *knocks.*

PETER: Knock knock.

SHANE: Hi Peter. Come in.

PETER: The door's locked.

SHANE: Oh sorry.

SHANE *opens the door for* PETER. BEN *is invisible to* PETER.

PETER: Dear, it's a warm morning. I think it's going to be a stinker.

SHANE *wraps his sandwich in Glad Wrap to give it to* PETER.

Have you packed some stuff?

SHANE: Yeah and I made you a sandwich... To have for lunch at the hospital.

PETER: Oh darling, you gem. I'm touched.

SHANE *puts* BEN*'s plate away.*

SHANE: Don't know why I got this plate out. I can't eat before the operation.

PETER: No, oh well. I'm making us something nice tonight.

SHANE: Cool.

PETER: Well, got everything?

SHANE: Think so.

PETER: Good. Okay then. Cab's outside.

PETER *exits.* SHANE *looks to* BEN *one last time.*

Brett Stiller as Ben and Sam Dunn as Shane in the Griffin Theatre Company production of STRANGERS IN BETWEEN, 2005. (Photo: Robert McFarlane)

PETER*'s bathroom. Later that day.*

SHANE *sees that* WILL *is present.*

WILL: He's all right, hey?
SHANE: Who?
WILL: Your friend. Peter.
SHANE: Yeah, Will, Peter's heaps good.
WILL: He likes to cook.
SHANE: Yeah.

SHANE *notices* WILL *is holding a towel.*

Are we going for a swim, Will?
WILL: No, you're having a bath. He just asked me to grab you a towel.
SHANE: Oh yeah. Thanks for letting me recover here. Your place is better.
WILL: This is Peter's place. Fuck, you're out of it.
SHANE: No. I'm cool.

PETER *enters. He runs the bath.*

PETER: I hope you'll be okay in here. You've got a towel. I only cleaned in here yesterday. I hope there's enough hot water. There should be.
WILL: This one's all over the place, Peter. You might want to keep an eye on him.
PETER: Who made me matron?
WILL: I'm the guest.
PETER: Do you feel okay?
SHANE: Yeah, it's just a bit hazy. Like nothing's real.

He looks to WILL.

I feel nice but.
PETER: You're on happy pills, darling.
SHANE: My arse hurts but, hey. Did you get the salt?
PETER: Oh yes. I popped down when you were under the knife or above the surgeon or whatever they did to you.

WILL *has found the salt.*

WILL: There you are.
SHANE: How much do I use?
WILL: Heaps.

WILL *punctures the bag and pours it in.*

SHANE: Is it expensive?

PETER: Seventy-four cents a bag.

SHANE: I'll pay you back.

PETER: No you won't.

SHANE *gets a bit light-headed as he leans over the bath.*

You right?

SHANE: Yeah. Is Will staying?

PETER: I think so. He likes my apricot chicken too much.

SHANE: It's nice you came, Will. [*to* PETER] We're not boyfriends but. We just wrestle on the couch sometimes. [*to* WILL] It's okay that we're not boyfriends.

PETER: It's a big city. You know what I say? You always fall in love with the first but it's the last you've got to hang on to.

SHANE: Yeah. Sorry I didn't finish your dinner. It was nice. I just felt like spewing.

PETER: Oh, thanks. It'll keep.

SHANE: I should have known I was allergic to the penicillin. See Mum knows those things. Not me.

SHANE *pulls off his top. It gets a bit caught on his head and* PETER *helps him.*

I hope I'm not allergic to anything else.

PETER *moves to the door.*

PETER: I could ring your mum.

SHANE: No.

PETER: Not to tell her about anything, just to check that you aren't allergic to anything else.

SHANE: She would think I was sick or hurt or something if you asked about that.

WILL: Maybe she would want to know that you're not.

PETER *gets a glass of water.*

PETER: I'll just pop that down there for you.

SHANE *leans over to test the water again. It hurts.*

SHANE: Fuck, I'm like an old man or something.

WILL: Want some help?

SHANE: I'll be all right.
PETER: All right. We'll leave you to it.

> PETER *and* WILL *go to leave.*

SHANE: Could you stay?
PETER: Sure.

> PETER *is careful to respect* SHANE's *privacy.*

SHANE: I won't be long. It will help me relax.
PETER: You'll feel better soon.

> SHANE *undresses. He has brown antiseptic around his shaved genitals.*

WILL: You right?

> *They help him into the bath.* SHANE *settles.*

SHANE: They shaved my nuts.
WILL: Did they?
SHANE: Yeah.
WILL: It'll grow back quick.
SHANE: The bath makes me feel better.
PETER: Good.

> SHANE *gives a tired smile.*

I'll put your dinner in a Tupperware container if you want.
SHANE: Okay. It was really nice.
PETER: It was one of Mum's recipes. She sent it to me years ago but I'd never made it. I found it the other day. It just fell out of the bottom drawer in the kitchen. About an hour before the phone call came through. Funny how things happen.
SHANE: When's the funeral?
PETER: Next Tuesday. I'm not going. It'll be too…
SHANE: You should. I'll go with you.
PETER: No, you can't afford that and…
SHANE: I want to. If it will help you.
PETER: It… would help. The plane trip home alone's what I'm dreading.
SHANE: Okay. Book us both a seat.
PETER: Okay.
SHANE: I'll pay you back.

PETER: No need.

SHANE: Maybe I could call my mum. I miss her.

PETER: Yeah, well, you could call her from here later.

SHANE: I won't tell her about this.

PETER: No.

SHANE: I'm scared my dad would answer.

WILL: They must be worried about you.

SHANE: Imagine if my brother answered.

WILL: That'd be good.

SHANE: No, he's not like you, Will.

PETER: You do what's best.

SHANE: Do you miss your mum?

PETER: I'm sad it couldn't have been better. I should have cared for her. That's the deal—they care for us when we're young and we care for them when they're old. No matter what happens in between, that's the deal. I didn't come through on my end of the bargain.

SHANE: I could call them and say I'm okay. I want to go back to school.

PETER: I'm glad.

SHANE: I wanna finish. Not there but. I can't. Here. I could find somewhere here. Maybe my mum would send me money.

PETER: We could work that out.

SHANE: I could do that. I could ring them later. Might be good if Ben answered. I might just go, 'I love you.' Wonder what he'd say to that. Could you please pass us the water?

PETER: Sure.

SHANE: [*taking the glass*] Thanks, Peter.

PETER: Good, Shane.

SHANE *drinks the water.*

THE END

Sam Dunn as Shane and Anthony Phelan as Peter in the Griffin Theatre Company production of STRANGERS IN BETWEEN, 2005. (Photo: Robert McFarlane)

Holding the Man

For Tim

Guy Edmonds as Tim and Matt Zeremes as John in the Griffin Theatre Company production of HOLDING THE MAN, 2006. (Photo: Toby Dixon)

Holding the Man was first produced by the Griffin Theatre Company at the SBW Stables Theatre, Sydney, on 9 November 2006, with the following cast:

TIM	Guy Edmonds
JOHN	Matt Zeremes
MARY-GERT, JULIET, RHYS, ROSE, A QUEEN, LOIS, HARRY, NIDA DIRECTOR, DOCTOR 2, GIA CARRIDES, YVES STENNING, SHRINK, VOICES, NIDA ACTOR	Jeanette Cronin
NEIL ARMSTRONG, SCARECROW, DICK, BOB, DERGE, QUEEN 2, WOODY, FRANCO, DOCTOR 1, PETER KINGSTON, NIDA ACTOR	Nicholas Eadie
PHOEBE, ERIC, BARTENDER, PHILIP, NIDA TEACHER, BEN FRANKLIN, VALERIE BADER, ANGEL NURSE, VOICES, NIDA ACTOR	Robin McLeavy
DAMIEN, MARIE, BISCUIT, LEE, DOOR BITCH, PETER, RICHARD, DAVID FIELD, NURSE 1, WAITER, DR SAM, FATHER WOOD, VOICES, NIDA ACTOR	Brett Stiller

Director, David Berthold
Designer, Brian Thomson
Costume Designer: Michael Agosta
Lighting Designer, Stephen Hawker
Composer and Sound Designer, Basil Hogios
Assistant Director, Nic Dorward

The following text went to press before the end of rehearsals, so may differ slightly from the play as performed.

CHARACTERS

TIM
JOHN

At home
DICK, Tim's father
MARY-GERT, Tim's mother
BOB, John's father
LOIS, John's mother

At school and college
DAMIEN
PHOEBE
JULIET
BISCUIT
DERGE
ERIC
RHYS

At university
LEE
WOODY
ROSE
PETER

In the theatre
NIDA DIRECTOR
NIDA TEACHER
NIDA ACTORS
PETER KINGSTON
GIA CARRIDES
DAVID FIELD
VALERIE BADER
YVES STENNING
BEN FRANKLIN

At the clinic and hospital
DOCTOR 1
DOCTOR 2
DOCTOR SAM
SHRINK (DR SHEPHERD)
NURSE
FATHER WOOD

Elsewhere
NEIL ARMSTRONG
HOUSTON MISSION CONTROL
SCARECROW
MARIE, Phoebe's mother
DOOR-BITCH
BARTENDER
QUEENS
HARRY, a one-night stand
PHILIP, a one-night stand
FRANCO, a lover
RICHARD, an AIDS patient
WAITER
MAIDS
ORDERLIES
ASSORTED VOICES

This adaptation was originally written for six actors: two actors playing Tim and John, and the remaining four playing all the other characters, with meaningful and appropriate doubling where possible. It could also be performed with a larger cast.

ACT ONE

On stage, on the night this play is being performed.

The actor playing TIM *enters and looks to the audience.*

ACTOR PLAYING TIM: Let's begin.

♦ ♦ ♦ ♦ ♦

The surface of the moon, 1969.

The Lunar Excursion Module casts a shadow. A small puppet spaceman enters. He is NEIL ARMSTRONG. *He is in conversation with the familiar voices and beeps of* HOUSTON MISSION CONTROL.

Meanwhile, TIM *is ten years old and sitting next to* DAMIEN *at school, in Melbourne, watching the TV.*

NEIL ARMSTRONG: Okay, Houston, I'm on the porch.

HOUSTON MISSION CONTROL: Roger, Neil. And we're getting a picture on the TV.

NEIL ARMSTRONG: I'm at the foot of the ladder. Going to step off the LEM now. That's one small step for [*Beep.*] man, one giant leap for mankind.

> DAMIEN *touches* TIM*'s leg. They whisper.*

DAMIEN: Is it really there? Tim, are they up there now on the moon?

TIM: Yeah.

NEIL ARMSTRONG: And Damien's touching my leg.

HOUSTON MISSION CONTROL: We missed that, Neil.

NEIL ARMSTRONG: Houston, he's touching my leg. Do you copy?

HOUSTON MISSION CONTROL: Roger, Neil. We're checking that.

DAMIEN: The teachers are crying. Why? They're crying.

> TIM *shrugs.* DAMIEN *puts his arm around* TIM.

HOUSTON MISSION CONTROL: We're getting a heart rate off the graph, Neil.

NEIL ARMSTRONG: Yeah. I know.

DAMIEN: Hold out your hand.

TIM: Why?

DAMIEN: Got a present for you.

> DAMIEN *drops a ball into* TIM's *hand.*

TIM: Kevin's superball. But it's his.

DAMIEN: It's a present. No one needs to know you've got it.

> DAMIEN *smiles and puts his lips to* TIM's *cheek.*

TIM: Don't.

DAMIEN: I wish you were a girl.

NEIL ARMSTRONG: Kind of stirring, a buzz coursing through me.

HOUSTON MISSION CONTROL: Roger, Neil. Just ride it out.

◆ ◆ ◆ ◆ ◆

Backstage at a shopping centre.

TIM *is alone. Enter an actor costumed as the* SCARECROW *from* The
Wizard of Oz.

SCARECROW: Who are you? You're not supposed to be backstage.

TIM: I'm Tim Conigrave.

SCARECROW: Who?

TIM: I am a friend of Phoebe's. She's in the centre court floorshow with
  you.

SCARECROW: Oh, you're Tim.

TIM: Yes, why? What have you heard about me?

> *Enter* PHOEBE.

PHOEBE: [*to* SCARECROW] Sorry, Bruce. Sorry about 'If I Only Had a
  Brain'.

SCARECROW: It happens. I know that. Anyone waiting for photos?

PHOEBE: Some.

> SCARECROW *exits.*

Tim, did you see me stuff up the dances?

TIM: Yes.

PHOEBE: You did?

TIM: Yes. I know them off by heart. No one could tell.

PHOEBE: They're more interested in their shopping list than me.

TIM: That's not true. You transport them.

PHOEBE: I think it's the escalator doing the work.

TIM: I want to cry in 'Somewhere Over the Rainbow' but I can't. I know why they talent-spotted you at the Maldon Fete, Phoebe.

PHOEBE: Thanks, Tim.

TIM: You made a lot of shoppers happy today.

PHOEBE: They're doing Shakespeare at your school with my school next year. You should audition with me.

TIM: Me? I couldn't do that.

PHOEBE: We'd spend more time together.

TIM: [*giving* PHOEBE *a kiss*] I'm sad I can't be your boyfriend, Dorothy.

PHOEBE: Oh look, I'm sick of this. Why do you have to make such an issue of it? There's more to you than being gay, but it's all you ever talk about.

TIM: You're the only person I can talk to.

PHOEBE: What's there to talk about?

TIM: Well…

PHOEBE: I mean, you say you're gay, I've said that's okay. Big deal.

TIM: I've been hiding this stuff for years.

PHOEBE: Half of my mum's friends are gay. My Aunty Shane is a lesbian.

TIM: I had to tell you because I went into such a spakko mood at the dance, outside, when we kissed, and I touched your breast and then went all quiet and then I wrote you that strange letter and I don't have feelings about girls, but the guys at school… All the time. That guy Rhys, you met at the dance…

PHOEBE: He had his girlfriend.

TIM: So did I.

Silence.

Sorry. There's also this guy, John. I don't talk to John. I never have. I noticed John on my first day at Xavier. Maybe it's because I'm at an all-boys school.

PHOEBE: Have you ever had sex?

TIM: Yes. With Kevin, a boy in my grade six class. I didn't really like Kevin. I liked Damien. He taught me to smoke and one time we like competed to tell the biggest lie in confession and… But Damien moved away in grade five.

PHOEBE: You did it in grade six?

TIM: Another time too. More recently. At the footy oval. Near my house.

PHOEBE: Who?

TIM: A man called Terry I met on a train.

PHOEBE: A man?

TIM: A boy. About eighteen. He had a boyfriend.

PHOEBE: He cheated?

TIM: They had an arrangement. Just as long as they didn't bring someone home.

PHOEBE: Oh.

TIM: I know. I wouldn't do that if I had a boyfriend.

PHOEBE: And did you just start talking on the train? How'd you know he was a gay?

TIM: Um. Well. I was coming home from the fundraising concert for the famine in Bangladesh at the Myer Music Bowl. We got talking about the bass player from The Little River Band. Terry led it. He was more experienced than me. He had a magazine with pictures of men kissing so it was pretty clear where we stood.

PHOEBE: I hope you weren't in danger.

TIM: No. Terry was nice. I liked that it felt dangerous a bit.

PHOEBE: No. You mustn't. People get abducted, Tim.

TIM: This guy John; he's really quiet and gentle but good at everything. I know it sounds dumb, but John's different. He has beautiful eyes, dark brown with these eyelashes.

PHOEBE: Will you see Terry again?

TIM: No.

PHOEBE: Was the concert good?

TIM: Mixed. Lots of glam and heavy rock. Too much Sherbet. I hate Daryl Braithwaite.

PHOEBE: He's okay.

TIM: Oh, you mustn't Phoebe. He's daggy.

PHOEBE: I like The Little River Band. Are they gay?

TIM: No. I would like the bass player to be.

PHOEBE: David Bowie is a bisexual. He likes men and women. Have you ever had sex with a girl?

TIM: No. Never.

PHOEBE: Maybe you should.

TIM: Something became clear to me once at the urinal of the change-rooms at Brighton Beach.

PHOEBE: You don't have to tell me everything, Tim.

TIM: Can't hurt. This surfie in board shorts was getting changed and I was standing there and I couldn't piss and I couldn't get him out of my head since and I dream about him still but that was years ago.

PHOEBE: Which guy?

TIM: Just some random. A random surfie in blue board shorts that I fell in love with out of the corner of my eye standing at a urinal this one time. It doesn't matter. John's shy but popular and really good-looking. He's captain of the Under-Sixteens.

PHOEBE: Well, I don't think he'll be...

TIM: No, I don't think he's gay. But what should I do?

PHOEBE: With what?

TIM: With John. Where do I go from here?

PHOEBE: Oh. Talk to him.

TIM: Talk to him. Can we be friends for ever, Phoebe?

PHOEBE: Yes.

TIM: I cried after we dropped you off. After the dance.

PHOEBE: Why?

TIM: Dunno. Just cried. Supertramp came on the radio and I hid my face from Dad and I cried.

PHOEBE: Yeah. I've gotta get changed. My plaits hurt. They do them really tight and they strap down my tits.

> *Enter the* SCARECROW.

SCARECROW: Pack of fuckwits, what would they know?

TIM: [*to* PHOEBE] I'll meet you out front.

> PHOEBE *exits.* SCARECROW *starts to get out of his costume. He has pale blue board shorts underneath.*

Must be terrifying in front of an audience. It was really good today but.

SCARECROW: Yeah, well, it pays the bills. I'm not really... I mean, a lot of my ideas weren't taken on board. Some. I went to NIDA.

TIM: NIDA. Really?

SCARECROW: Bit different on the other side of the fortress so don't believe everything you hear. I left after second year so, because it can be limiting—that's the decision I made—but I mean, I also do voice-overs and write but this isn't really me because I'm saving up to go to the States. Phoebe says you think you might be gay.

TIM: What? She told you?

SCARECROW: Yes.

TIM: That's our secret.

SCARECROW: I'm a bit of a role model for her and the others. I only wanted to say, mate, don't you think it's a bit early to make that decision? You're only fifteen, aren't you?

TIM: It's not really a decision.

SCARECROW: You've got your whole life ahead of you is all.

TIM: I know.

SCARECROW: Do you have doubts?

TIM: No. Not any more. I have unrequited fantasies.

SCARECROW: Which is sweet but just don't close off your options. That's kind of a motto for me.

TIM: Okay.

SCARECROW: Okay.

♦ ♦ ♦ ♦ ♦

A classroom.

JOHN *is doodling at a school desk. If* JOHN *engages with* TIM, *it is only brief and comes from politeness rather than genuine interest.*

TIM: Is this… Is someone sitting here?

JOHN: Nup.

> *Silence.*

TIM: Do the homework?

JOHN: Yep.

TIM: Me too. Difficult?

JOHN: Nup.

TIM: Geography sucks.

JOHN: 't's all right.

TIM: Yeah. It's all right.

> *Silence.*

I'm in a play with your brother. Seniors' Shakespeare.

JOHN: Oh yeah?

TIM: Yeah. *Romeo and Juliet.*

> *Short silence.*

The Most Excellent and Lamentable Tragedy of Romeo and Juliet.

JOHN: Boring?

TIM: No. It's a love story.

> JOHN *glances up from his doodling.*

JOHN: Playin' Romeo?

TIM: No. The competition.

JOHN: Who?

TIM: Paris, the one Juliet leaves for Romeo.

JOHN: Poor Paris.

> *Silence.* JOHN *doodles.* TIM *tries to sneak fleeting glances at* JOHN.

TIM: You're up for the APS Best and Fairest.

JOHN: Think I've ruined my chances. Argued with a ref. Which team do you play for?

TIM: I play soccer.

JOHN: A soccer choc.

TIM: Used to play firsts basketball. I'm Tim.

JOHN: John.

TIM: Yeah.

JOHN: Better pay attention.

> *Silence.* JOHN*'s pencil case is in reach.* TIM *gives into the urge and scrawls across it.* JOHN *looks at* TIM*'s graffiti.*

[*Reading*] 'U shall win'?

TIM: The Best and Fairest medal.

JOHN: Oh. 's a new pencil case.

TIM: Sorry.

JOHN: No, 't's okay.

> TIM *finds another pencil case. It is* JOHN*'s pencil case eighteen years hence. It is covered in their graffiti.* TIM *reads from it.*

TIM: [*unheard by* JOHN]

'There's hope for the living and hope for the dead,
But there's no hope for John 'cause he's gone in the head.'
Your handwriting, 'If it feels good and hurts no one, do it!' And another time, I wrote: 'John has asked me to stop writing on his pencil case, so I won't do it any more. See, I've already stopped.' This went on for ages.

TIM *returns to his seat and swaps the new pencil case for the relic.*

[*To* JOHN, *a whisper*] Hey, congrats, hey.

JOHN: Thanks.

TIM: On your trophy.

JOHN: Yeah.

TIM: I need to update your pencil case. Not 'U shall win'.

TIM *scribbles out the word 'shall' on the pencil case.*

'U win.'

JOHN: When's your play?

TIM: Thursday and Friday.

JOHN: You must be nervous.

TIM: Shitting myself.

JOHN: Poor Paris.

TIM: Are you coming?

JOHN: Don't know much about theatre.

TIM: I thought you'd be coming 'cause your brother's in it.

JOHN: Guess I should try. Thursday maybe.

TIM: [*aside*] Beaudy.

◆ ◆ ◆ ◆ ◆

The foyer of Xavier school hall after the show.

Enter DICK *and* MARY-GERT, TIM's *dad and mum.*

DICK: Here he is. Larry Olivier.

TIM: I forgot my lines.

DICK: Oh no, we wouldn't have noticed except for the prompt you got.

MARY-GERT: I don't think I did notice.

DICK: Yes, you said…

MARY-GERT: Oh no, I was just caught up in the emotion of it all.

DICK: Yes. Really good.

TIM *is craning to spot* JOHN.

MARY-GERT: Who are you looking for, Tim?

TIM: No one.

MARY-GERT: Do you have to see a teacher before we get away?

Enter PHOEBE *and her mum,* MARIE.

TIM: No.

PHOEBE: Hi Tim.

TIM: Hi Phoebe.

PHOEBE: This is my mum, Marie.

TIM: Pleased to meet you. These are my parents, Mary-Gert and Dick.

DICK: You must be very proud of your daughter.

MARIE: Yes. Lovely.

DICK: Few shaky flowers at the cemetery.

MARY-GERT: Dick.

DICK: But very good.

MARY-GERT: [*to* MARIE] Weren't they lovely? Pleased to meet you.

> *As the parents talk,* TIM *and* PHOEBE *have their own separate conversation.*

PHOEBE: [*to* TIM] D'you sign my program?

MARIE: [*to* MARY-GERT *and* DICK] Lovely, yes.

TIM: [*to* PHOEBE] Yeah.

DICK: [*to* MARIE] Yes.

PHOEBE: [*to* TIM] Did he come?

MARY-GERT: [*to* MARY-GERT *and* DICK] The costumes…

TIM: [*to* PHOEBE] It was John I was imagining dead…

MARIE: [*to* MARY-GERT *and* DICK] Lovely.

TIM: [*to* PHOEBE] …at the graveside…

MARY-GERT: [*to* MARIE] Yes.

TIM: [*to* PHOEBE] …to make me cry on stage…

MARIE: [*to* MARY-GERT *and* DICK] Yes.

TIM: [*to* PHOEBE] …and he couldn't even bother to show.

MARY-GERT: [*to* MARIE] All the emotions, I thought. It had all the emotions.

PHOEBE: [*to* TIM] Maybe he'll come tomorrow.

MARIE: [*to* MARY-GERT *and* DICK] Lovely, yes.

PHOEBE: [*to* TIM] It'll be better then.

DICK: [*to* MARIE] Yes it was very well done.

TIM: [*to* PHOEBE] Yeah.

MARY-GERT: [*to* MARIE] Yes.

PHOEBE: [*to* TIM] I want to do plays for ever.

MARIE: [*to* MARY-GERT *and* DICK] Lovely.

PHOEBE: [*to* TIM] We could have a dinner.

MARY-GERT: [*to* MARIE] Yes.

TIM: [*to* PHOEBE] Have to be girls there.

MARIE: [*to* MARY-GERT *and* DICK] It's important, I think.

MARY-GERT: [*to* MARIE] Oh yes, terribly.

PHOEBE: [*to* TIM] Juliet and me.

MARIE: [*to* MARY-GERT *and* DICK] Yes.

PHOEBE: [*to* TIM] Your place…

MARY-GERT: [*to* MARIE] Good socially too.

PHOEBE: [*to* TIM] …Wednesday night…

MARIE: [*to* MARY-GERT *and* DICK] Yes, lovely for them.

PHOEBE: [*to* TIM] …I'm cooking.

MARY-GERT: [*to* MARIE] Yes.

PHOEBE: [*to* TIM] Invite John.

DICK: [*to* TIM] Well, we should get going, you've got school tomorrow, son.

TIM: [*to* PHOEBE] You're so pushy.

MARY-GERT: [*to* MARIE] They work them hard.

PHOEBE: [*to* TIM] It'll work out.

MARIE: [*to* MARY-GERT *and* DICK] Work them very hard, yes.

MARY-GERT: [*to* MARIE] Lovely to meet you.

MARIE: [*to* MARY-GERT *and* DICK] Yes, you too, yes.

DICK: [*to* MARIE] See you then.

MARIE: [*to* MARY-GERT *and* DICK] Lovely, yes.

PHOEBE *and* MARIE *exit.*

MARY-GERT: Well, she was lovely.

DICK: Phoebe's a pretty girl, Tim.

MARY-GERT: Very good actress, I thought. All the emotions.

♦ ♦ ♦ ♦ ♦

A locker room.

BISCUIT *and* JOHN *are selecting their books for the next class.*

BISCUIT: Ah, fuck. Have we got fuckin' Latin now?

TIM *approaches.*

JOHN: [*to* BISCUIT] Yeah.

TIM: Hi John.

JOHN: Hi. I'm sorry I wasn't there on Friday. How did it go?

BISCUIT: Err, just fuckin' talk to him and ignore me, Conigrave, why don'tcha?

TIM: Hi Biscuit.

BISCUIT: G'day.

TIM: It went okay. Good actually.

JOHN: Paul said the cast party was pretty good.

TIM: [*aside*] Better if you'd been there, John. [*To* JOHN] Was pretty good.

BISCUIT: Err, bumchums.

TIM: Shut up.

JOHN: I was out on a run and when I got back there was this note from Mum saying that she and Dad had gone to Paul's play.

BISCUIT: Err fuckin' *Homeo and Faggiet*.

JOHN: That's when I remembered. Sorry. Better get off to Latin.

BISCUIT: I thought you were boyfriends with me, Conigrave.

TIM: [*to* BISCUIT] Sorry, Biscuit, my heart belongs to John. [*Aside*] My God.

BISCUIT: That's cool. We'll make it a triangle.

JOHN: I'll see you at the break. Come on, Biscuit.

TIM: [*aside*] What, is that just a throwaway?

BISCUIT: Give us a gander at your homework, Caleo?

TIM: And John, I'm having an end-of-term dinner on Wednesday night with Phoebe and Juliet from the play. D'you wanna come?

BISCUIT: Don't play favourites, Conigrave.

JOHN: [*to* TIM] Getting home might be a bit difficult.

TIM: [*aside*] Stay over. [*To* JOHN] Phoebe lives over your way. I'm sure you could get a lift with her.

JOHN: Sounds good.

BISCUIT: [*to* TIM] We'll talk about this in bed, pumpkin. [*To* JOHN *as they leave*] I'm good at being a gay, hey.

>   JOHN *and* BISCUIT *exit.*

TIM: [*aside*] John Caleo at my place for dinner and… Fuck. Maybe he's only coming to meet some girls. Fuck.

♦ ♦ ♦ ♦ ♦

TIM*'s place and time races and whoosh, enter* PHOEBE *and* JULIET.

JULIET: We wanted to get here before lover-boy.
TIM: Fuck.
JULIET: It's all right, darling, I knew from the moment I met you.
　　　Fuck, the doorbell rings.
TIM: [*aside*] Fuck. Doorbell—a bolt of lightning—his silhouette through the glass—schoolbag over his shoulder—dressed quite formally.
JOHN: I got lost on the way from the station.
　　　JOHN *hands over a bottle of lime juice and a bottle of soda water.*
TIM: [*aside*] Introductions. [*To* JOHN] Phoebe played Juliet—Juliet played Lady Montague—I played Paris. [*Aside*] Silence—the girls stare.
　　　Glasses of lime and soda have been distributed in an instant.
JULIET: You and Tim are at school together?
TIM: [*aside*] Disbelief at an obvious question—silence again—John fumbles with his glass.
PHOEBE: What did you think of the play?
JOHN: I didn't see it.
PHOEBE: We were fabulous.
TIM: [*aside*] Silence—fuck—food comes out.
　　　PHOEBE *has served the food at an electric pace.*
PHOEBE: [*delegating places*] Juliet and me there. John next to Tim here. Dig in.
　　　Whoosh, enter MARY-GERT.
MARY-GERT: It's only me. Won't disturb you. Promised to hide. Oh! That's an interesting seating arrangement.
TIM: [*aside*] More introductions—my mum—agonising crap—she wants to say something unimaginably embarrassing…
MARY-GERT: Such ruddy cheeks still.
TIM: [*aside*] Try…
MARY-GERT: Didn't notice he got a prompt.
TIM: [*aside*] Surprise me.
MARY-GERT: I once made the terrible mistake of serving asparagus hors d'oeuvres at a piss party.

TIM: [*aside*] Mum ushered away.

> MARY-GERT *has gone.*

PHOEBE: We're a new group of friends, so we should pass a kiss around the table as a kind of bond.

TIM: [*aside*] Terror fuck—a plan afoot—I'm next to John—he'll refuse —Juliet and Phoebe—kiss—linger—wish I was a girl—Phoebe up for air, then…

> *Silence for the first time in the scene.* PHOEBE *and* TIM *kiss.* TIM *slams his hand onto* JOHN*'s leg.* JOHN *moves his hand onto* TIM*'s.* TIM*'s eyes light up.* TIM *turns as* JOHN *shuts his eyes and purses his lips.* TIM *presses his mouth against* JOHN*'s. They kiss.* TIM *breaks free as* JOHN *opens his eyes. They catch sight of each other.* JOHN *grows a small, almost undetectable smile. We hear a snapshot of the girls' applause as time accelerates again.*

PHOEBE: Bravo.

JULIET: Sweet. Last but not least.

> *Wham,* JULIET *throws her arms around* JOHN *and gives him a smacker on the cheek. Fuck, there's that alarming fuckin' doorbell again.*

TIM: [*aside*] Doorbell before long enough.

> *Whoosh, enter* MARIE.

Marie, Phoebe's mum, is a taxi home.

MARIE: Lovely, yes, sophisticated, lovely, all very lovely. Yes. Lovely. Well then…

TIM: [*to* JOHN] Glad you could come and um, I'll see you tomorrow at school tomorrow.

JOHN: Sure.

TIM: Cool. Yeah, um [*a quick peck on the cheek*] goodbye.

JOHN: Bye.

> *Suddenly all but* TIM *and* PHOEBE *have gone.*

PHOEBE: [*a kiss on* TIM*'s cheek*] He's divine.

TIM: [*whispering*] Do you think he's gay?

PHOEBE: It doesn't matter. He obviously likes you and that's all that's important.

> TIM *is alone.*

TIM: [*aside*] There goes the boy I've kissed. Marie, his life is in your
    hands. I better not hear you've had a head-on with a tram.

◆ ◆ ◆ ◆ ◆

The Caleo's. A phone rings. Enter BOB CALEO.
The Conigrave's. TIM *is at home. Simultaneous.*

*A note here about the phone conversations. Handsets are non-essential
and the phone conversation should not inhibit interaction between the
two speakers.*

TIM: Hello Mr Caleo, can I speak to John, please?
BOB: Whom may I say's calling?
TIM: Tim. Tim from school.
BOB: John! Phone.

    Enter JOHN.

    [*To* JOHN] Mate from school. [*To* TIM] 'Tim'?
TIM: [*to* BOB] Tim.
BOB: [*to* JOHN] Tim.
JOHN: [*to* BOB] Tim? Oh?

        BOB *exits.*

    Hi Tim.
TIM: Oh hi. It's Tim.
JOHN: Nice surprise.
TIM: So—good—um—there's something I want to tell you.
JOHN: I'm all ears.
TIM: This game that… you know this stupid triangle game that Biscuit's
    been playing? It's been going on and on and today he was going on
    about how I have to drop you and I don't want to. I'm being serious.
    What I'm trying to say is I like you.
JOHN: That's good.
TIM: I… I really like you. I've liked you for some time.
JOHN: I like you too.
TIM: Does this mean we're going out together?
JOHN: You haven't asked me yet.
TIM: John Caleo, will you go round with me?
JOHN: Yep.

TIM: Oh.

> *Silence.*

Have you ever had a girlfriend?

JOHN: One.

TIM: I think I knew I was gay when I was eleven.

JOHN: I don't know if I do know if I am.

TIM: That's okay. Bi is better. Bowie is bisexual. Do you like Bowie?

JOHN: Mmmh. I've always wanted to be married with kids. I want kids.

TIM: I'll have to be their godfather.

> MARY-GERT *leans in.*

MARY-GERT: Tim, please, you've been on the phone for ages, please.

TIM: Yep, Mum. [*To* JOHN] How do you, how do you reckon your family and stuff would react?

JOHN: Mmmh, not good.

TIM: No.

JOHN: Yep. And whatever happens, like, however things turn out, we'll always be friends. Let's agree to that.

TIM: Yeah, let's.

> MARY-GERT *pokes her head in.*

MARY-GERT: Please, Timothy. You have been on the phone for two hours. Please. Truly.

TIM: Okay, okay. [*To* JOHN] Did you hear that?

JOHN: Has it really been two hours?

TIM: Better go.

JOHN: I'll see you tomorrow.

TIM: Sleep well.

JOHN: You too.

TIM: I don't want to hang up.

JOHN: Me neither.

TIM: This is it, I'm hanging up.

JOHN: You didn't hang up.

TIM: Nup. Sweet dreams, my boyfriend.

JOHN: Goodnight.

♦ ♦ ♦ ♦ ♦

Kings Domain, Melbourne.

TIM *and* JOHN *are together.*

TIM: [*unheard by* JOHN] I reached out and touched your hair. You turned and kissed my hand. You smelt like soap and clean clothes. Gentle. Little angel kisses. If this had been it, if I had died then, I would have said it was enough.

   JOHN *catches* TIM *daydreaming.*

JOHN: What?
TIM: [*to* JOHN] I can't believe this.
JOHN: What?
TIM: This. I've liked you for ages and here I am sitting in Kings Domain with you, holding hands. I would never have thought it could happen.

   They pash.

[*Aside*] Phoebe was right, you can tell when a boy has an erection.

   TIM*'s hand dives into* JOHN*'s pants.*

JOHN: We better get back. I'll miss my train.
TIM: Yep. Sure. Hang on but. My, um, stiffy is all… Just need to wait a sec. I'm so turned on I'll have to go straight home and pull myself.
JOHN: You don't do that, do you?
TIM: Are you joking?
JOHN: I don't think it's good for you. Why do you need to do it?
TIM: It's fun.
JOHN: Why don't you see if you can stop?
TIM: Okay.

     ◆ ◆ ◆ ◆ ◆

A classroom.

JOHN *has a letter from* TIM.

JOHN: [*reading*] Dear John, it's Tim, it's four-thirty in the morning and I can't sleep. I'm confused about what happened at the park. I think I went too far too soon when I undid your dacks.
TIM: [*unheard by* JOHN] I was so rapt, I would have done anything for

you but God alone knew how. I was ready to blow in my jocks there and then.

JOHN: [*reading*] All I can say is I'm sorry. I don't want to put pressure on you to have sex or anything like that, especially if you don't feel ready.

TIM: [*unheard by* JOHN] Every night in bed, hands above the covers, wondering if pulling myself might jinx things between us.

JOHN: [*reading*] If all we ever do is hug, that is enough for me.

TIM: [*unheard by* JOHN] Dear God, please don't have me called to the blackboard. I am so hard.

JOHN: [*reading*] When I give you this letter, I won't say anything. When you are ready, talk to me.

TIM: [*unheard by* JOHN] Finally I read *Cleo*, by accident, and I tried but there was a sexy saxophonist in the Daly Wilson Big Band and I just brushed my erection but…

JOHN: [*reading*] Yours sincerely, Tim.

TIM: [*unheard by* JOHN] …I'm sorry, John.

JOHN: [*to* TIM *in a whisper*] Everything's all right.

◆ ◆ ◆ ◆ ◆

A school corridor.

BISCUIT *reads from a copy of* Sursum Corda.

BISCUIT: *Sursum Corda*: Xavier College Students' Magazine. Profiles of New College Prefects. 'Name: Caleo, John. Best Friend: Tim. Highest accolade: 1976 Best and Fairest. Hobbies: Anything that involves Tim. Favourite Colour: Essendon black and red or anything Tim is wearing.'

    BISCUIT *exits.* JOHN *approaches* TIM.

JOHN: Did you read *Sursum Corda*?

TIM: I saw. I don't care.

JOHN: My profile. They know.

TIM: Oh, that? Doesn't matter.

JOHN: Walks a thin line, Tim.

TIM: It's not malicious, John. In a way it's kind of accepting. Father Lewis reckons the staffroom gossip's always about you and me.

JOHN: You've spoken to Father Lewis about us?

TIM: He worked it out. All the Jacks did. He reckons whatever we do we'll do in dignity.

JOHN: Why hasn't someone tried to stop us?

TIM: Lay staff want to but the Jesuits look out for us. Seen it all the time.

JOHN: Jesus.

TIM: Lewis says only magical people get talked about. I'm not in *Sursum Corda*, John. In your profile, but not the chosen twelve.

JOHN: No. Are you okay?

TIM: Course I am, yeah. Doesn't matter. I only wanted prefect so I could turn it down—to make a stand. I think it's revolting to set one group of boys apart, give them power and ask them to dob on their mates. It's just a form of policing.

JOHN: Not everything has to be political.

TIM: And they always choose the guys who excel at sport. I find the whole thing elitist.

JOHN: And…

TIM: And congratulations; the coffee scrolls are on me at lunch. I can't believe I didn't get one; ye bastard.

JOHN: Good.

TIM: Lewis was cool. Been thinking he could come talk to my parents…

JOHN: About us?

TIM: Well, if you don't think…

JOHN: No way, Tim. Father Lewis.

TIM: Okay. Geography?

JOHN: We have a prefects' meeting.

TIM: Oh.

>   JOHN *exits.*

♦ ♦ ♦ ♦ ♦

A slumber party.

DERGE, TIM, ERIC, RHYS *and* BISCUIT *bounce on in sleeping bags.*

BISCUIT: I fucked the cunting English exam. I answered all three fuckin' questions. Meant to select two. I've fucked Comprehension.

TIM: You knew to choose two.

RHYS: That was in all the fuckin' trials.

BISCUIT: I know. That's what I'm saying. I fucked it. I fucked it up the arse.

DERGE: Fuck it.

BISCUIT: I know. Fuck it. I don't care. What's fuckin' done's fuckin' done.

TIM: Fucking HSC. Hate waiting for fucking results.

BISCUIT: Shut up, Conigrave. All school I've hated you fucks saying you're scared of a fuckin' result, you're smart, fuck off.

TIM: No. Just. Waiting's the worst. Shut up, Biscuit.

ERIC: Can't believe it. School's fuckin' gone now.

TIM: You heard about the talent scout?

RHYS: What?

TIM: John's been selected by the Essendon Under-Nineteens.

BISCUIT: Fuck.   ERIC: That's great.

DERGE: Fuckin' deserves it too.

TIM: That's why he couldn't come up here. He's going to a training camp.

RHYS: Listen to you. Like his fuckin' wife. Or mum. Like his fuckin' mum.

TIM: [as Lois Caleo] Well, I'm proud's all.

BISCUIT: Might mean he might play for Essendon one day.

TIM: He will.

DERGE: Your mum and dad's fuck ranch is really nice, Eric.

ERIC: Fuck off.

RHYS: Thanks for having us up here.

ERIC: That's all right. Don't call it a fuck ranch, please. I've been coming here since I was two. It's our holiday house.

RHYS: They would fuck here a lot.

ERIC: Shut up, please.

DERGE: Hey, what's the most bizarre sexual thing you've heard of?

RHYS: Um, farm boys get the poddy calves to suck them off. Poor calf wants milk and it gets a mouth full of spoof.

TIM: Poor calf.

BISCUIT: Well, a Wesley guy cut the mut out of a porno poster and put mince meat behind it and shoved it in a bar heater to keep it warm and…

DERGE: That was you, Biscuit.

BISCUIT: Bull-fuck. Piss off.

TIM: How do youse wank?

DERGE: Hey?

RHYS: Backhand.

DERGE: What?

TIM: We all do it. I sort of pump the bed like I'm fucking it.

ERIC: Making baby beds.

BISCUIT: That's kind of what I do. Leave my jocks on and then put a flannel down the front and pump it.

RHYS: Don't you share your bedroom with your brothers?

BISCUIT: I can cum without making a noise.

TIM: I can cum quietly. I've cum at slumber parties with youse before.

DERGE: Fuck off.

TIM: I've cum at camps and retreats and shit. I've probably cum with youse in the room a thousand times.

ERIC: Yeah, me too.

DERGE: Sometimes.

ERIC: I rub the head of my cock, that's my favourite way.

RHYS: Sometimes I do it nasty-fast like I'm feeding really hungry chooks.

ERIC: I rub my bell-end with my thumb and finger really fast until I cum. I think I might do it now.

Silence. They each start wanking in their sleeping bags. After some time…

TIM: Um. So this is weird.

DERGE: Shhh.

Quiet batting.

ERIC: We should race to see who can cum first.

TIM: You're saying that 'cause your way's so efficient.

ERIC: Yep.

Quiet batting.

BISCUIT: I've wanked three times a night since I was fourteen, no matter where I was.

TIM: Still two more to go tonight.

BISCUIT: Just one. I did it before in the toilet.

ERIC: Better fuckin' of fuckin' cleaned it up, filthy fuckin' mongrel.

TIM: As if the walls of this place aren't already dripping with cum.

ERIC: Shut the fuck up; I'll snap.

DERGE: Shhh. I'm concentrating.

> *Quiet batting.*

TIM: I thought about cuming so now I'm going to cum.

ERIC: Oh. Me too.

> ERIC *and* TIM *cum.*

DERGE: Spose I better too.

ERIC: Give him some privacy, Conigrave.

TIM: How?

ERIC: Look at the fuckin' floor or something.

> DERGE *wears his orgasm face.*

TIM: Looks like the planet's blowing up when Derge goes.

> DERGE *is cumming.*

DERGE: Phew. Far out.

RHYS: No. Nup. Na. No. Oh. Fuckin' dirty slut. Ohh.

> RHYS *cums and is suddenly silenced by shame.* BISCUIT *is still wanking.*

DERGE: A good stress release.

TIM: I wanked so much during the HSC.

ERIC: Oh, red raw.

DERGE: C'mon, Biscuit, you can do it.

BISCUIT: Shut up.

ERIC: I hated not seeing anyone during study break. That was the worst HSC thing.

TIM: My worst HSC experience… I was studying, one night, late, heaps late and my dad comes in and he puts his arm around me and he cries.

ERIC: When you're ready, Biscuit.

BISCUIT: Shut up, will you?

DERGE: What do you mean, Tim?

TIM: He cried.

DERGE: Why?

ERIC: Stress. It's even stressful for parents. My whole house turned upside down.

BISCUIT: Okay, okay, fuck, fuck, okay, fuck.

BISCUIT *roars.*

TIM: Quietly, hey?

BISCUIT: Oh man.

ERIC: Your brothers must be deaf.

BISCUIT: Oh, Jesus fuckin' Christ.

> *They continue their conversation with half an eye on* BISCUIT *who is emerging from the throes of ejaculation.*

DERGE: Tim, how come your dad cried?

TIM: I dunno. He doesn't accept me.

BISCUIT: [*finally resurfacing*] What's to accept?

TIM: Thanks, Biscuit. Circle-jerk buddies accept each other.

RHYS: We are completely not circle-jerk buddies.

ERIC: Yeah.   BISCUIT: Goes without saying. We're not, I
                                                       mean.

TIM: John and I are.

> *Silence.*

John and I are lovers.

BISCUIT: Youse two? I knew. I knew it.

TIM: Did you?

BISCUIT: I knew that.

ERIC: I didn't. Never thought… It's good but. It's okay that yez are, you-knows.

TIM: Thanks. That's why my dad cried.

RHYS: You told them?

TIM: I refused to go on a family trip to Sydney so I could spend time with John and they asked why.

DERGE: What'd they say?

TIM: Dad said I'd grow out of it because boys do sexual things with each other sometimes…

ERIC: We don't.

TIM: And Mum said if I don't grow out of it, I'll have a sad and very lonely life. I got Father Lewis to talk to them.

BISCUIT: Lewis?

ERIC: [*to* BISCUIT] Oh, he's not one, is he?

TIM: No. Maybe. He told Mum to make some new house rules and now John sleeps in the sunroom and we wait for them to be asleep before he sneaks into my room.

RHYS: And they're okay now?

TIM: I thought so until Dad goes, 'Please don't do this to us' and dripped tears all over my homework.

DERGE: What'd you do?

TIM: Nothing. I just sat there and rubbed his arm. What could I do? I've never seen my dad cry. And he kind of wiped his tears and said sorry and went out.

DERGE: Well, the circle-jerk brothers don't mind. You and John. We don't care.

BISCUIT: Yeah. You and John.

ERIC: Yep.

TIM: Thanks, boys.

BISCUIT: So do youse arse-fuck and stuff?

ERIC: Biscuit.

TIM: Um no, we haven't done that.

ERIC: Biscuit, I can't believe you asked.

ERIC, BISCUIT, RHYS *and* DERGE *exit.*

♦ ♦ ♦ ♦ ♦

At home.

DICK *and* MARY-GERT *are waiting up. A cask of riesling is handy.*

DICK: Could you come in here, son?

TIM: Just a minute, Dad.

DICK: Can we see you, please?

TIM: [*aside*] Doesn't sound good.

TIM *approaches his parents.* DICK *takes a deep breath.*

DICK: You and John can't see each other any more.

TIM: Yes we can.

DICK: His father was in my office this morning, waving a pack of letters at me and yelling that you corrupted his son, a good Catholic boy, trying to make him homosexual.

TIM: What?

DICK: He made me read one letter. Something about you putting pressure on John to have sex.

MARY-GERT *tops up her glass of wine.*

TIM: Where the hell did he get that?

MARY-GERT: While John was staying here last night Mr Caleo went through his room. He obviously expected to find something. He accused your father of being a party to the whole thing.

TIM: He has no right to go through John's stuff.

DICK: Don't you understand? You're not to see each other. The man's threatening court action.

MARY-GERT: Who knows what he'll do next time.

TIM: And do you support him?

DICK: You listen, Tim. We've been good to you but this morning was the most humiliating moment of my life. You hear?

TIM: We're adults now. We're at uni.

DICK: Living under our roof.

TIM: You can't stop us.

MARY-GERT: Of course we can't. We can't stop you, Tim. But John won't be staying here any more and you won't be invited to the Caleos'.

DICK: And you can't use the phone to contact him.

TIM: [aside] Sometimes you smash doors and furniture. But sometimes you grit your teeth and say with quiet disgust… [To MARY-GERT and DICK] Fucken' poxy traitors, I hope you get cancer. [Aside] Then slam the door and yell, so all the neighbours can hear… [To MARY-GERT and DICK] Fucken' poxy cunts. [Aside] And that's what I did.

◆ ◆ ◆ ◆ ◆

Catholic Girls' College, Monash University.

Enter JULIET, *above.*

TIM: Juliet? Juliet?

JULIET: What?

TIM: I need to use your phone.

JULIET: Tim, the nuns will shit if they find you here. They'll think you're from the boys' college.

TIM: Do you have a phone in your room?

JULIET: Come in.

TIM: It's an emergency. It's John.

JULIET: What's wrong?

TIM: I need you to ring him. Our parent's have banned us.

JULIET: Arseholes.

TIM: Poxy cunts. I called mine poxy cunts. John's dad went to my dad's work. It's… I cried all the way here.

JULIET: You poor things.

TIM: I need you to call him. They won't suspect a girl.

JULIET: Yeah okay, you dial, but if the nuns catch you, you're dead.

TIM: I just came here 'cause I was on campus and I knew you'd help.

JULIET: Mannix boys get chased out every night. There's an eighty-five per cent marriage rate between here and them.

> TIM *sees* JOHN *and* BOB *approach the stage.*

TIM: It's dialling.

> *Enter* BOB *before* JOHN.

BOB: Hello.

JULIET: Hello, it's Juliet calling. May I please speak to John, please?

BOB: One moment, Juliet.

JOHN: [*softly*] Hello…

JULIET: Tim just told me. He wants to talk to you.

TIM: Bubby. Are you okay?

> JOHN *tries to say 'yep' but chokes on tears.*

We'll get through this.

> JOHN *tries to say 'yep' again but tears stop him again.*

We'll be okay. I… I love you.

> BOB *is lurking.*

JOHN: [*unvoiced*] I love you too. [*Whispers*] I'd better go.

TIM: Bye.

JOHN: Bye.

> JOHN *exits.*

TIM: Oh shit.

JULIET: Poor boys.

TIM: You know what pisses me off? Us being together never hurt anyone but it's okay for that dickhead to destroy his own son.

JULIET: Come on. I'll sneak you out through the chapel.

◆ ◆ ◆ ◆ ◆

Monash University campus.

LEE, *who we will soon know as a campus activist, reads from the Monash University Student Newspaper.*

LEE: *Lot's Wife*: Monash Uni Student Rag, 1978.
   Dear Editor,
   I am gay and I am surprised by the current level of anti-gay thinking on this campus and even in my own house. Gays are just like everyone else. My boyfriend is gay and he was captain of the football team at school. He isn't like the gay stereotype. He is strongly built and masculine, and if you were to meet him you wouldn't know he was a gay. We have been together for three years, which is longer than most of our non-gay friends' relationships. Our parents would argue it's wrong because gay sex doesn't produce babies. Where does that leave infertile couples? Our parents would say it's unnatural, but so is having a haircut or driving a car. We love each other. Tim. First-year medicine.

   The University Quad. TIM *is sitting next to* ROSE *with* LEE *and* WOODY. *They have milkshakes.* TIM *has the student newspaper.*

WOODY: I just wish members would stop casting themselves in Shakespeare and propose a show that would actually challenge the status quo.

LEE: Bourgeois shits.

WOODY: Academia versus practical revolutionary theatre, you know what I mean?

TIM: Have you read this letter in *Lot's Wife*?

WOODY: Completely politically naïve.

TIM: Isn't it.

LEE: So how's *Blithe Spirit* going, Tim?

TIM: I'm just operating the poltergeist effects but everyone can see me running around in my blacks. I hope I get a role where I'm supposed to be seen soon.

LEE: You will. Student theatre's totally democratic.

TIM: Thanks for the milkshake, Lee.

LEE: 't's okay.

TIM: I wrote that letter in *Lot's Wife*.

WOODY: You?

LEE: I thought you were doing Science.

TIM: I didn't feel brave enough to sign my real name.

LEE: Some poor first-year med student just got outed.

WOODY: Are you really in a relationship like that?

TIM: Exactly like that.

LEE: Must have been a baby when you met. It's so sweet.

WOODY: It's so encouraging. It's what we're fighting for.

TIM: Where?

WOODY: At Gaysoc.

TIM: What's Gaysoc?

WOODY: I thought that's why you were sitting here.

LEE: Haven't you come here for the meeting?

TIM: What meeting?

LEE: Campus Gays. You must join.

TIM: If it means I'll meet other gay people because I only know you
    guys from the drama society.

WOODY: Well, there is some crossover with the drama society.

LEE: It's just me and Woody.

WOODY: And Rose.

LEE: Oh yeah. Have you met? This is Rose.

TIM: Hello.

> ROSE *nods.*

WOODY: So, the minutes should show we started at one thirty-four
    p.m.

LEE: …With the struggle for the betterment of gay and lesbian life on
    the table…

WOODY: Woody presiding, Lee as secretary…

LEE: And where's the mini skirt I was promised?

WOODY: Don't be sexist.

LEE: Was I?

WOODY: Borderline. And Tim. We have our new member Tim.
    Welcome.

TIM: Thanks.

LEE: And we all have swampwater milkshakes because I'm so
    generous.

WOODY: Lime and chocolate, who would have thought?

LEE: Thank you.

WOODY: Keep the receipts.

LEE: They're on me.

WOODY: Good. So. Sexuality Week. Lee will you report on Gay Blue-Jeans Day?

LEE: Yes. It's going to happen.

WOODY: And say what it is.

LEE: Well, Woody, everyone who's gay will be invited to wear blue jeans to uni. Most people wear them anyway, so everyone has to make a choice that might force them to consider their prejudices and it is a fabulous idea.

WOODY: It's brilliant.

LEE: We would also like to have a couple kissing in the lift in the Menzies building.

WOODY: But we don't have one.

LEE: Rose knew some girls. But they broke up.

>   ROSE *nods*.

And they still said they won't.

>   ROSE *sighs*.

Woody? You and Peter?

WOODY: It should be Monash students.

LEE: Well, there has to be someone. What about Tim and his boyfriend?

TIM: No. I don't think so. And he's over at RMIT.

LEE: Well, there are eighteen thousand kids on campus and if we believe the statistics of one in ten that means nearly two thousand gay guys. And girls. So where are they? And don't say the library toilets.

WOODY: It's too confronting for them to come to a group like this.

TIM: The guy, in the board shorts, over there? Maybe he's here for the meeting.

WOODY: Probably a breeder on a dare.

TIM: He's waiting for something. We're not very visible…

LEE: Except for your jaw on the floor.

TIM: We should say hello.   ROSE: Would you…

TIM: [*to* ROSE] Pardon?

ROSE: Would you care so much if he wasn't so good-looking?

TIM: Well… You might have got me there but…

ROSE: Or if he was a lesbian?

TIM: [*as Queen Victoria*] Surely that's not possible.

ROSE *tips her milkshake over* TIM *and storms off.*

LEE: Will we still have a quorum?

WOODY: We've never had a quorum.

TIM: I don't understand what I did wrong. It was a joke. Queen Victoria.

LEE: Sorry. We let you walk right into that.

WOODY: Rose's big beef is lesbian invisibility. Your comment only confirms it.

LEE: I'll just put she left the meeting early.

WOODY: Name her.

LEE: Of course I'll name her. 'Rose.' What's her surname?

WOODY: It'll come to me.

TIM: I should apologise.

WOODY: Leave it. She's just had a very bad time being gay. When she told her parents, her father asked her if she wanted to be a man.

LEE: He had her committed.

TIM: That's outrageous. Poor Rose.

WOODY: It's amazing she isn't more fucked up.

LEE: Actually, she is pretty fucked up.

TIM: You know what I think would be good? People need to talk to each other. We're all having a bad time. Should have it together. If there was a number to call, literally, pick up the phone. I know the union counsellor. She could train us. We could answer calls. [*Aside*] My first meeting and I was elected to co-chair a subcommittee.

◆ ◆ ◆ ◆ ◆

PHOEBE's *house.*

JOHN *runs to* TIM *and* PHOEBE.

PHOEBE: Here he is.

JOHN: Fuck.

TIM: John? You came.

PHOEBE: We didn't know where you were, John.

JOHN: I ran.

TIM: You're sweating. Did you run the whole way?

JOHN: I ran. I bolted. I'm dead. I'm fuckin'… Dad and I had a fight. What am I doing here? He'll work out I'm here. He knows you're here, Tim.

TIM: What can he do? Phoebe's mum's making us dinner.

JOHN: I should go back. He knows you're a friend of Phoebe's. He'll work it out, Tim.

>   JOHN *kicks something.*

TIM: John…

JOHN: I just cracked. I've never spoken to him like that, never spoken to anyone like that. I called him an arsehole, Tim. I told him if he can't accept you and me, I don't want him to be my father and then I just took off.

TIM: I think that's good.

JOHN: It's my dad. Don't say that. It's my dad, Tim.

>   *Enter* MARIE *being menaced by* BOB CALEO.

BOB: Is this Phoebe?

MARIE: This is her mother speaking. Hello.

BOB: This is Robert Caleo. John's father.

MARIE: Oh, hello Robert. Now we've found John. He's standing right here.

>   *As* MARIE *gives the game away,* PHOEBE *makes pantomime signals telling her not to.*

But. No. He's not.

BOB: Is Tim there?

MARIE: Tim? Oh.

>   *The signals grow.*

Lovely. Well…

BOB: Do you realise there are homosexuals at your dinner table?

MARIE: Oh. Look, I don't think it's any of your business, Robert. You're being a fool. My beetroot soup is ready to serve and I'd prefer that you didn't ring here again. Goodnight.

>   BOB *exits.*

I'm sorry, John, but your father is a very rude and irritating man.

JOHN: Sorry.

MARIE: No, that's all right, love. I'll make up the spare room for you both. It's only a single bed, I'm sorry.

>   MARIE *exits.*

JOHN: I won't be able to stay, Phoebe.

PHOEBE: You must stay. You've done the hardest part.

PHOEBE *exits*.

TIM: You can stay here tonight, you know.

JOHN: Dad'll be waiting up.

TIM: Serves him right, don't you think?

JOHN: I know it's wrong, but I really enjoyed giving him the shits today.

TIM: Stay.

JOHN: Okay.

TIM: Will you marry me? Err, why did I say that? That just fell out.

JOHN: It's nice. You're a dick but it's nice, Timba.

TIM: Timba? I like that.

♦ ♦ ♦ ♦ ♦

A union office.

WOODY *is on a beanbag opposite* TIM.

WOODY: Might be a problem with the phone.

TIM: I tested it.

WOODY: It might take some time before people feel empowered enough to call.

TIM: Oh okay.

WOODY: Yeah.

TIM: I told John about the Homosexual Conference.

WOODY: Oh good. Will he come?

TIM: He's even keen to get a gay group started at his college.

WOODY: Queer group.

TIM: Oh okay. I think it's his dad. He's getting political. Empowered.

WOODY: My boyfriend doesn't get it. Peter thinks activists are just angry people. I organise rallies; he invites friends to tennis parties.

TIM: John's sporty. You don't hear of many sporty gay guys.

WOODY: Gotta keep fit.

TIM: Woody, you know when you're making love…?

WOODY: Do you mean fucking? You're talking about anal sex?

TIM: Have you done it?

WOODY: Many times. I think it's important. Men being intimate or being penetrated challenges the patriarchy.

TIM: Oh okay. Yeah…

WOODY: Have you?

TIM: John screwed me for the first time last night and I found it painful. I'd done it to him but this time he did me and it would hardly go in and it felt like I needed a shit.

WOODY: It takes practice, my friend. You've just got to relax. I get Peter to chew my earlobe. It distracts me and before I know it, he's in.

TIM: Weird. John too.

WOODY: Might have to meet John.

TIM: Thanks for that.

WOODY: It's a counselling line after all.

TIM: Wish the phone would ring.

> *The phone doesn't ring.*

One more thing, my bum wouldn't close and the cum kept dribbling out for about half an hour.

WOODY: Your sphincter was probably in shock. It'll get used to it.

TIM: It's a bit sad to have lovemaking with John reduced to dick-in-the-bum mechanics.

WOODY: Fucking. Call it fucking.

TIM: I would like you to meet John.

WOODY: Can I have a hug?

> WOODY *leaps on* TIM.

TIM: Woody, you're crushing me.

> WOODY *nuzzles* TIM's *neck.* TIM *lets him.*

WOODY: Sorry.

> WOODY *starts to kiss* TIM. TIM *doesn't kiss* WOODY *back.*

What's the matter?

TIM: You said a hug. I'm in a relationship. And so are you.

WOODY: Peter and I aren't monogamous.

TIM: But isn't that what a relationship is?

WOODY: It's not fair to expect our lovers to fulfil all our needs. Peter likes to play tennis and I don't, so he plays with other people. Why can't sex be like that?

TIM: Keeps you fit.

WOODY: I think you'd like Peter. Sinewy and lithe—a seriously sexy man.

> TIM *and* WOODY *are drawn closer as they fantasise about their boyfriends.*

TIM: John is the most beautiful man I have ever seen. His chest is round and his eyes are like chocolate.

WOODY: Mine's Mediterranean too.

TIM: I don't think I could ever go to Italy—it might kill me.

WOODY: Catholic boys' school must have been interesting. Did you have a sexual relationship then?

TIM: Yes.

WOODY: Do you remember the first time?

TIM: Of course.

WOODY: I had an erection for most of my schooling.

TIM: Father Wallbridge organised a retreat to Barwon Heads. John and I put our sleeping bags together and nuzzled noses. He smelled so sweet. I remember exchanging breath and his puffing. I made him cum twice and he said he felt like he'd played a grand final. I wrote a poem the next day about two suns—exchanging atmospheres—drawn into each other—spiralling into each other.

They are close enough to kiss.

WOODY: Can I kiss you?

TIM: No. You can't.

WOODY: Okay.

♦ ♦ ♦ ♦ ♦

A gay bar.

JOHN *and* TIM *loiter at the entrance.*

DOOR-BITCH: Hi boys. Five dollars, please. Hold onto your raffle ticket; there's a lucky door prize.

TIM and JOHN venture in.

Daisy, tell me you saw those eyelashes. And they're real.

Mirror balls and dancing gays for days.

TIM: My God.   JOHN: My God

TIM: I didn't expect it to look like this.

JOHN: Where do we sit? There?

TIM: No, they're kissing there.

JOHN: Don't stare.

TIM: Shit.

JOHN: Over near the bar.

TIM: They're actually all gay men.

JOHN: Well, yeah.

TIM: Let's start talking to people.

JOHN: What, 'We're Tim and John and we'd like to be your friends'?

TIM: I want to go up to them and say, 'So, do your parents know? How did they take it? Tell me about your life?'

JOHN: Looks like a lot of their parents wouldn't be still alive.

TIM: That one that looks like David Cassidy. I'd like to know about him.

JOHN: He dances like he's in *Disney on Ice*.

A QUEEN *has approached.*

QUEEN: You boys new here?

JOHN: Yes.

QUEEN: Didn't think I'd seen you. I'm sure I'd remember.

A BARTENDER *pops up.*

BARTENDER: What can I get you girls?

JOHN: Us? Oh. Beer?

BARTENDER: Drinks at the other bar. We do toasted sandwiches and coffee.

JOHN: Oh.

A second QUEEN *drifts by.*

QUEEN 2: Grab a hot buttered man on toast, sweets.

BARTENDER: Fresh out, lovey.

QUEEN 2: Oh. Story of my life.

BARTENDER: Ooh ah. Barbra Streisand Babs Babs.

QUEEN: Babs Babs, darling. *A Star is Born*. Such a sell-out. Quack quack darling la la, Ducky.

BARTENDER: Oh, I know. Mmwa mmwa tee hee ha ha Babs Babs Judy Judy vagina.

JOHN: [*to* TIM] What are they talking about?

DOOR-BITCH: Raucous.

TIM: [*to* JOHN] I don't know.

QUEEN: Huge.

JOHN: [*to* TIM] Should we dance?

QUEEN 2: Rock-Hudson-dizzy-bitch-fist.

TIM: [*to* JOHN] People will stare. Should we stay?

> *All the* QUEENS *and* MEN *cackle.*

DOOR-BITCH: Ra ra Babs Babs…

BARTENDER: …I've just got time to show you my pussy…

QUEEN: …Ohh hoo hoo.

> *The* Are You Being Served? *lift pings. A 'Benny Hill' chase clears the stage.*

♦ ♦ ♦ ♦ ♦

TIM*'s car, later that night.*

JOHN *is in the passenger seat.* TIM *is flicking through* The Advocate, *a US gay newspaper. Silence.*

TIM: I'm a bit disappointed.

JOHN: It was a bit strange.

TIM: Not how I expected.

JOHN: No.

TIM: I wanted masculine men to run up—strut up—and invite us to meet their friends.

JOHN: Not likely…

TIM: Not a bunch of scowling fruits sneaking furtive looks at each other. Maybe it is a sad lifestyle.

JOHN: Stay.

TIM: What?

JOHN: Stay tonight.

TIM: No way. At least I got this [*the newspaper*]. Imagine.

JOHN: A gay newspaper.

TIM: Queer newspaper. That's what you say.

JOHN: Stay. Mum and Dad don't get back from the beach house until Monday. You can if you want.

TIM: No way. Shut up. [*Reading*] This thing is what Woody said… There's something called Gay Cancer.

JOHN: Boring. So are you going to stay?

TIM: No. I'm not.

JOHN: Stay in case I die of Camp Cancer before morning.

TIM: No. You're crazy. What if they come home early?

JOHN: They never do. Please.

TIM: Oh, let's just do it in the car.

JOHN: It was your grandma's, so no. And I injured myself on the gear stick last time.

TIM: Incorporate it.

JOHN: And the horn goes and the blinkers come on. It doesn't work so just stay.

TIM: I… I just hope your father hasn't installed Tim-detectors. [*Unheard by* JOHN] That night, we made love like we were reclaiming old territory.

◆ ◆ ◆ ◆ ◆

JOHN*'s bedroom.*

A car door slams and morning snaps on. Enter LOIS *in the kitchen.* TIM *and* JOHN *scramble in the bedroom.*

LOIS: Paul, bring in the blue bag, please.

JOHN: Shit. Mum. Put your clothes in the cupboard.

LOIS: The blue bag in the boot, please.

JOHN: Get in the cupboard too.

TIM: Really?

JOHN: Really. Do it.

TIM *hides.*

TIM: [*from within*] It's happening. I can't believe it.

JOHN *enters the kitchen.*

JOHN: Mum.

LOIS: Hello dear. Will you help your brother get the things in, please?

JOHN: Mum. Tim's here.

LOIS: John…

JOHN: He's upstairs.

LOIS *tightens her lips.*

Is Dad here?

LOIS: Probably on his way in. He went to put the bins out.

JOHN: Sorry.

LOIS: Look, you'd jolly well better get Tim out. Not very happy about this.

JOHN: Don't tell Dad. Please, Mum.

LOIS: Look, truly, I think the whole thing's absurd but don't disobey your father.

JOHN: We are in love.

LOIS: I don't judge you, John. I'm just afraid. I'll go busy your father with something or other.

JOHN: Thanks.

♦ ♦ ♦ ♦ ♦

The Fifth National Homosexual Conference.

TIM *is wearing a T-Shirt that reads 'Uranium: not a good look— Monash Gaysoc'. The actor playing* TIM *has a new wig: something longer and hippier.*

TIM: [*unheard by* JOHN] We climbed the stairs toward the Universal Workshop foyer at Monash. You took my hand and held it proud and secure as we entered The Fourth National Annual Homosexual Conference. [*To* JOHN] Now don't mention Peter to Woody.

JOHN: Why?

TIM: They broke up.

JOHN: No?

TIM: Keep up; our friends are sluts. Peter's seeing this gorgeous guy Ian.

JOHN: We're playing tennis with Peter next weekend. The barbeque at Clifton Hill.

TIM: Don't mention that to Woody. We want to stay unaligned in the break-up.

> TIM *has a conference brochure.*

It's an ugly brochure. Organised by self-loathing nannas lecturing us for taking freedom for granted—I'll hate that. Although... [*Reading*] 'Get Your Filthy Laws Off My Body: A Practical Forum On Being Young and Gay in 1980.' Least that'll be full of spunks.

> TIM *folds the brochure.*

Feel like I'm missing out on the thrill of the hunt sometimes, John.

> JOHN *gives* TIM *a look.*

I mean... Well... I'm nearly twenty-one and you know... I'm

worried that we're missing out on what people in our generation are supposed to be experiencing. They all go on about it... Screech Beach changing sheds. Saunas. Trade.

JOHN: Tim, are you trying to hurt my feelings?

TIM: I feel sexually inexperienced. Don't you feel that? You've only had sex with me.

JOHN: I don't want to have sex with other people.

TIM: Okay. But would you allow me to?

JOHN: I don't know why you'd want to. Is there something about me?

TIM: I don't believe it's fair to expect our lovers to fulfil all our needs.

JOHN: Where d'you read that?

TIM: An open relationship isn't a sin, John.

JOHN: I don't want to talk about this. Not here in public.

> JOHN *exits*.

TIM: [*aside*] I think that was a no. We joined a newly formed collective called 'Young Gays'. It *was* full of spunks.

◆ ◆ ◆ ◆ ◆

A tennis pavilion.

JOHN *storms in, racquet in hand.*

JOHN: I'm out of sight so you just...

TIM: No. John...

JOHN: What were you doing with Ian just then?

TIM: I was just feeling his nipple under his overalls. I know it looked bad but...

> *Whack!* JOHN *punches* TIM *in the stomach.*

John. John, I wasn't doing it to hurt you. It's just... I can't believe you punched me, John.

> TIM *coughs as he recovers.*

JOHN: Tim, after our discussion the other day I did some thinking and I was coming round to what you suggested. But not if you're going to flaunt it like that. Now everyone thinks I don't satisfy you. You know how that makes me feel?

TIM: John, please. I'm just a bit pissed and... I never thought you'd...

JOHN: I never thought you'd... Have anyone. That's what you want.

TIM: I'll drive you home.

JOHN: Peter has his car. Drive Ian home.

TIM: Will you call me?

JOHN: I might let you sweat it out a while.

TIM: [*aside*] That's fucked that. I am so stupid sometimes.

> JOHN *exits.*

In my search for adventure, however, I did start trolling.

♦ ♦ ♦ ♦ ♦

A party.

Enter HARRY.

HARRY: Do you have the time?

TIM: It's eleven.

HARRY: Are you a poofter?

TIM: Um yeah.

HARRY: This is my first gay party. God, if my parents knew! In their country, in Turkey, they used to stone people for being gay.

TIM: I'm pretty stoned.

HARRY: I'm just drunk on being here. I can't believe how many good-looking guys there are. What time is it?

TIM: Twelve thirty.

HARRY: I've missed my train.

TIM: I live in St Kilda in a share house. I have a spare mattress.

HARRY: I have to get home before my parents wake up.

TIM: It's two. How early do they get up?

HARRY: Six. Still two hours. Does anal sex hurt?

TIM: Only at first.

HARRY: I'm a virgin and I reckon you'd be gentle with me. Cool house.

TIM: You're sweet, but I have a boyfriend.

HARRY: He's not here. You don't think I'm attractive.

TIM: I'm trying to resist. Believe me.

HARRY: I'm getting ball cramp waiting all this time.

TIM: [*aside*] I screwed Harry. He had no trouble doing what, for me, had been a painful thing. In fact he enjoyed it immensely. [*To* HARRY] Have you done this before? Was this all a con-job?

HARRY: Come off it. Shit, my parents will be up in a second. Bye.

> HARRY *exits.*

> *Inflation Nightclub. Enter* PHILIP *in an elaborate eighteenth-century costume and powdered wig. He is a New Romantic.*

PHILIP: Hi.

TIM: Hey.

> *Silence.*

First time here?

PHILIP: No.

TIM: Cool.

PHILIP: I always come to the New Romantic nights at Inflation.

TIM: Cool.

PHILIP: Lee told you I liked you, hey?

TIM: No.

PHILIP: He did. I do.

TIM: Oh. [*Aside*] Philip was clearly an experienced lover. He manoeuvred himself around my cock with obvious expertise. But again I sensed that something was missing. I didn't know what.

PHILIP: So do you want to go out with me?

TIM: No.

PHILIP: Why?

TIM: It was really nice but I don't think we should. I couldn't bear it if my boyfriend found out.

PHILIP: Maybe you should have thought about that before you led me on all this time.

TIM: I didn't lead you on. I was honest the whole way.

PHILIP: Cunt rash.

> PHILIP *exits.*

> FRANCO*'s bedroom. Enter* FRANCO, *choosing a cassette for his player.*

TIM: All I ever do is upset people.

FRANCO: What would your boyfriend do if he found out? This is my getting-ready music.

TIM: Part of me wants to share it with him, Franco.

FRANCO: Come off it. Christ, we're gonna be early at this rate.

TIM: He's my best friend. I've shared everything with him. You look good in my shirt.

FRANCO: This whole month behind his back?

TIM: I can't. He'd be so disappointed. He's so devoted. It makes me nervous. Oh, I can't wear this. He loves me so much, everyone says that, but I feel obligated to him and I want craziness.

FRANCO: Sounds like you've got some issues there, mister. When my boy gets back from overseas he won't know shit. Shit, let's wait. I don't want to be on time.

TIM: Knowing that this, you and me, was always going to be finite has made it so intense.

FRANCO: You wanna fuck again, hey.

TIM: Yep.

FRANCO: Me too. We're late anyway.

> *They pash.*

> *A party.* PETER *sits near* TIM. *They share a joint.*

PETER: Where's John tonight, Tim?

TIM: What'd you say, Peter?

PETER: Is John coming later?

TIM: Wanna go upstairs or something, Peter? Party's too loud.

PETER: I'm right. So John still not here?

TIM: Has some nerdy chiro assignment.

PETER: You're still together?

TIM: Yeah.

PETER: Yeah.

TIM: You heard we had a fight at your tennis thing?

PETER: Yeah.

TIM: Yeah.

PETER: Yeah and you seem to be coming onto me on the dance floor all night.

TIM: Yeah.

PETER: Yeah.

TIM: Thinning out now. I might go home soon. Wanna come round for a drink?

PETER: Sure, but not for sex. I couldn't do it to John.

TIM: He doesn't have to know. You're not rejecting me, are you?

PETER: I wouldn't feel right about it.

TIM: Oh. Okay. Don't tell him I asked, hey.

> PETER *exits.*

◆ ◆ ◆ ◆ ◆

TIM's *house in St Kilda.*

TIM *and* JOHN.

JOHN: Tell me, Tim.
TIM: What?
JOHN: There's something on your mind.
TIM: Not now.
JOHN: Just say it. There's something…
TIM: It's not something I want to say in bed.
JOHN: Don't torture me, Tim.
TIM: I need some space.
JOHN: What's that mean?
TIM: We've been together for five years and I'm starting to lose my identity. I'm no longer Tim but part of John and Tim.
JOHN: What's wrong with that?
TIM: I want to go to acting school next year and there are just things, things that I want to do that wouldn't involve you.
JOHN: You mean sex with other men.
TIM: I mean a separation. A trial separation.
JOHN: How long for?
TIM: A couple of months.
JOHN: When does this start?
TIM: Well, I don't know…
JOHN: Now?
TIM: Well, yes, I guess it has to start now.
JOHN: I see.
TIM: Are you okay about it?
JOHN: No, why would I be? Can I still sleep here tonight?
TIM: Of course. I'm not going to kick you out of my bed.
JOHN: Well, if it's started I can…
TIM: No, stay tonight.
JOHN: Yeah. I would prefer to stay tonight.
TIM: Yeah. Stay tonight but then tomorrow we'll start a separation.
JOHN: Tomorrow we start?
TIM: Starts tonight but stay tonight. If you like. I don't…
JOHN: A trial though.
TIM: Yeah, for a set time. A few months.
JOHN: No more Tim and John.
TIM: Just for a few months.

JOHN: It doesn't mean we can't cuddle.

TIM: I think it does.

> JOHN *turns his back on* TIM.

[*Unheard by* JOHN] I hoped to God you wouldn't start crying. Later, Phoebe told me you cried daily. [*Aside*] He looks so cute, his little ear sticking out. I can't bear hurting him like this.

> TIM *places a hand on* JOHN. *He shrugs it away.*

[*Unheard by* JOHN] I lay awake for ages.

> JOHN *takes* TIM*'s hand and wraps himself.*

♦ ♦ ♦ ♦ ♦

The National Institute of Dramatic Art, Sydney, an audition room.

All actors to the stage as CANDIDATES *watching* TIM.

DIRECTOR: Tim, mate, good. When you're ready we'll hear your monologue. You look tired, mate. When you're ready. Don't be nervous.

TIM: Okay. Ready?

DIRECTOR: Ready, mate.

TIM: [*beginning*] When the phone…

DIRECTOR: Sorry, mate, before you start. We saw you last year, didn't we?

TIM: Yes. Told me to come back.

DIRECTOR: Just wanted to check. When you're ready.

> TIM *recites the following as his monologue.*

TIM: When the phone call came, things shook. 'Tim, you're in.' I'm in. I am in. An actor friend from Anthill says, 'That's good, turtle, if that's what you want.' What I want? Is she mad? I wanted to tell everybody, the woman in the café, the old man in the street, but I also didn't want to appear to be bragging. 'A cappuccino, thanks, and by the way, I just got into NIDA.' [*As a friend of his mum's*] 'Very proud. Mum just told me, you've been accepted into Narnia.' Narnia? For fuck sake. It's the school Mel Gibson went to and Judy Davis. Not the lion and the witch. Mel Gibson. Judy Davis. For fuck sake. You must have heard of it? I went and got a crew cut. A new start. Regrowth.

> TIM *removes his wig to reveal a crew cut.*

The monologue becomes a duologue between JOHN *and* TIM
at TIM's *flat. The kettle and the popcorn are mimed as if they
are performing the scene in a rehearsal room at NIDA. The*
DIRECTOR *and* ACTORS *remain on stage observing.* JOHN's *hair
has reached its 1980s height.*

JOHN: I don't know if I like your hair.

TIM: Number two. I like it. Cup of tea? I'm making popcorn. Want
some?

    TIM *starts the detailed business of making a cup of tea.*

JOHN: Just tea. Please.

TIM: Kettle's on.

    TIM *makes sure the kettle is on at the wall.*

[*It was*] So dumb barely seeing you the past month. Surprised you
came. Glad you came. Just busy packing and…

JOHN: I came to congratulate you. Phoebe told me.

TIM: Thanks. I'm over the moon.

JOHN: We made you something. I'm not going to see you much, am I?

TIM: I'll be coming back from Sydney for the term breaks.

JOHN: Guess so.

    TIM *tends to the popcorn.*

So, been seeing someone.

TIM: You have?

JOHN: Yeah.

TIM: Anyone I know?

JOHN: Peter.

TIM: Lucky you. He's sweet. And very cute. I tried once but he couldn't
do it because of you. That's what he said.

JOHN: He told me.

TIM: Have you slept together?

JOHN: A couple of times. Mostly we play tennis.

TIM: What's he like in bed?

JOHN: You're not even jealous.

TIM: No. I'm not. Is that why you told me?

JOHN: Maybe. I don't know. Yes.

    TIM *pours the kettle into the popcorn.*

TIM: I think it's great, a chance to experience something different.

JOHN: Did you just…? You just poured the kettle into the popcorn.

TIM: Yes. I did.

> *They share a laugh.*

JOHN: Oh. Don't go away.

> TIM *completes the task of disposing of the popcorn and preparing the cup of tea for* JOHN *and himself. He wipes up after himself as he talks.*

TIM: Come off it. What about Peter?

JOHN: Dad scared him off anyway.

TIM: Bob? Finally on my side.

JOHN: I'll miss you too much.

TIM: I'm shit scared. I know that I'm going to rock up and then they'll go:

DIRECTOR: 'Hey, listen, I thought Tim Conigrave was the boy with the blond curly hair not the poof trying to look masculine in James Dean gear.' Sorry, mate. Keep on going.

> TIM *nods to the* DIRECTOR *and stumbles to recall his next line in the scene.*

TIM: Probably, ah, maybe I just fluked my way in on the day.

JOHN: You're such a worry-wart. We made you this.

> JOHN *produces a scrapbook.* TIM *puts down his tea and looks through it. The scrapbook is the first real object in the scene.*

This is what we made you.

TIM: What's… 'This Is Your Life—actually only the last five years.' How did you get all this together?

JOHN: The others pitched in. Biscuit did the section of skating stacks.

TIM: Classic.

JOHN: Down the freeway ramp. Phoebe had the pickies of the plays.

> JOHN *sips his tea—careful, it might still be hot.*

TIM: And Christmas Eve on the Yarra. Phoebe, Juliet—all with commentary—your handwriting. Thank you. Thanks, John.

JOHN: No wuckers.

TIM: I want to make one for you.

JOHN: Like you'll have time in the next three years.

TIM: What am I getting myself in for?

JOHN: I want to buy you something.

TIM: What?

JOHN: A ring.

TIM: A ring?

JOHN: Yeah. A ring. A kind of memento to say thanks for the last five years.

TIM: Well, I'd like to buy you one too. Most couples give each other rings at the start of the relationship, and here we are, doing it when we break up.

JOHN: Are we breaking up?

TIM: Well…

JOHN: I thought we were just separating, a trial, just seeing other people.

TIM: I think NIDA's changed that. It'll be hard to maintain anything over such a distance. I'm sorry, John, but don't you think the relationship was winding down? It was getting a bit stale.

JOHN: Oh well, I guess I knew it was coming. Let's get on a tram. I don't want to go home. Come out. We'll catch a tram. Let's go to Inflation. Wednesday's Gay Night.

They have put down their cups of tea.

♦ ♦ ♦ ♦ ♦

Inflation Nightclub.

Depeche Mode's 'Just Can't Get Enough' is playing. JOHN *takes* TIM*'s hand, dragging him onto the dance floor.*

TIM: It's like we're on our first date.

JOHN: Pardon?

TIM: Nothing.

JOHN: Hey?

TIM: I want to kiss you and tell you I love you…

JOHN: I can't hear.

TIM: …because I do but saying it now would make things harder for you.

JOHN: I can't hear you, Tim.

TIM: I know. Doesn't matter. I do love you, John Caleo. [*Aside*] We bought the rings. I put mine on my wedding finger.

END OF ACT ONE

ACT TWO

The National Institute of Dramatic Art, Sydney.

ACTORS *are in black lycra, warming up on stage for a movement piece.*

TEACHER: On the count of three, form a new friendship. One. Two. Three. Now separate. Form a new friendship. And separate. Form a new one. Good. Keep that repeating, okay, for three years.

AN ACTOR: Rolling.

AN ACTOR: Undressing.

AN ACTOR: Talking.

AN ACTOR: Feeling.

AN ACTOR: Mingling.

AN ACTOR: Sweating.

AN ACTOR: Farting.

TIM: Nothing left to hide.

TEACHER: Roll on the floor. And cry. Cry on a neighbour. Good. And totally breaking down. Okay, shake it out. Very good. Thoughts?

AN ACTOR: Um, it's like the friends you make here will be your friends for life.

TEACHER: Anyone else feel that?

ALL: Yes.

AN ACTOR: And it's like, it's like some people have a block with anger.

TEACHER: Okay, good, choose an animal and just…

AN ACTOR: I'm a monkey.

AN ACTOR: I'm a monkey.

AN ACTOR: I'm a chimpanzee.

AN ACTOR: I'm a Central African fruit-gathering gibbon.

> *Everyone's a monkey and very excited. They fight and fuck as monkeys do.*

TEACHER: Um, Tim, effeminate monkeys don't get work.

> TIM *masculinises his monkey.* JOHN *emerges.*

JOHN: How's NIDA?

> TIM *stops being a monkey. The* ACTORS *become a car. It's a hot day.*

TIM: It's all I talk about.

JOHN: Oh.

> TIM *watches* JOHN *adjust the rear-vision mirror—an* ACTOR*'s hand—and shift the gear stick—another* ACTOR*'s foot. The actors also provide the hum of the engine.*

TIM: I can't escape it. How's chiropractics?

JOHN: I'm doing pretty well. We can stop at a servo soon if you want.

TIM: Cool. Good to have someone to drive home with.

JOHN: I wanted to check out Sydney. No air-conditioning, sorry.

TIM: I'll make air-conditioning with my coffee cup.

> TIM *winds down the window, an* ACTOR *provides the handle and noise, another* ACTOR *blows the incoming breeze.* TIM *shovels air in with his empty coffee cup.*

JOHN: You're still mad.

TIM: John, you deserve better than me and I don't deserve you at all but I would like us to get back together, if you'll have me back.

JOHN: Good.

TIM: Bit understated.

JOHN: No. I think that's good.

TIM: Right.

JOHN: My parents want me to stay in Melbourne but, maybe, when you graduate we should try living together, maybe.

TIM: In Sydney?

JOHN: I guess.

TIM: But, and, like that's sensible and all, to stay apart, I mean the phone calls alone and long-distance relationships don't work; so like we'll… While we're apart we can have sex outside the relationship.

JOHN: So it's a relationship.

TIM: Yeah. But apart.

> *The car drives away without* TIM. TIM *fucks the nearest male* ACTOR.

FUCK ACTOR: So I said to Betty, I'm not coming to voice class if we can't take our shoes off.

TIM: Sorry, can we just, sorry, NIDA's all I talk about, and…

FUCK ACTOR: Sorry, yeah, keep on fucking me.

TIM: Thanks.

AN ACTOR: Rolling.

AN ACTOR: Swinging.

AN ACTOR: Listening.

AN ACTOR: Feeling.

AN ACTOR: Rooting.

AN ACTOR: Drinking.

AN ACTOR: Spewing.

TIM: Nothing left to hide.

AN ACTOR: And it's like, it's like some people have a block with pop psychology.

TEACHER: Anyone else feel that?

ACTORS: No.   TIM: Yes.

TEACHER: Work hard, Tim. And don't wear those sneakers so much. You came up at a heads of department meeting and we don't think they let your feet breathe.

TIM: No, okay, thanks.

TEACHER: Breathe.

> *A breathing exercise. A monkey screams. An* ACTRESS *drinks from a cup.*

ACTRESS: [*aside*] For my voice. I have nodules.

TIM: Can I've a sip?

ACTRESS: You can have it; I don't want any more.

TIM: Are you afraid that you might catch…

ACTRESS: No.

TIM: I don't have AIDS. Even if I did, you can't get it from sharing a drink.

> *The* ACTORS *scurry from* TIM *as screaming monkeys, ending the NIDA movement piece.*

◆ ◆ ◆ ◆ ◆

On stage, The Stables Theatre, Darlinghurst, Sydney, 1985.

TIM *addresses members' night.*

TIM: My name's Tim. Tim Conigrave and, um, I'm a new member here at Griffin, the Griffin Theatre… Company, and I think it's really good that someone like me can just get up and say my idea at Members' Night… tonight. I just graduated from NIDA, the class of '84, so I know some of you… I have seen some really interesting things here and even though the seats are so uncomfortable, you don't notice, um, but some of you are fidgeting so just… I'm just talking too much, um… I'll be down in the foyer with you all so just talk to me, um, if you don't think my thing is shit. But what I'm proposing is a devised response, like I'm not a writer, I'm an actor, but like a response to HIV/AIDS which will… because the media doesn't deal with stories about people affected except the sex-death-horror shit, which is fucked, and maybe we can do something. And I heard this military general talking about the Namibian Border War on Radio National and he called civilians soft targets and maybe a good working title for this project could be *Soft Targets*.

A VOICE FROM THE AUDIENCE: Sounds a bit like an anus.

TIM: Oh well, maybe you'd prefer *Fuck Me Dead*, Paul, ye f… I'll see yez in the foyer.

◆ ◆ ◆ ◆ ◆

A Sydney living room.

Enter RICHARD, *an AIDS patient, a grotesque and giant puppet with an empty frame and sharp sunken cheeks, half-bed half-man, coughing and spluttering.*

RICHARD: Sorry, yuck, I'm so clammy.

TIM: Thank you for… Thanks for taking the time…

RICHARD: You right sitting on the bed?

TIM: Fine.

RICHARD: I have night sweats.

TIM: We are asking people…

RICHARD: Long as you're comfortable.

TIM: Yes. The cast and I made some set questions for our research that we…

> RICHARD *has a coughing fit. Though we might not notice,* TIM *holds his breath.*

RICHARD: I hate having to take morphine. I hate the taste.

TIM: What's it for?

RICHARD: For headaches that nothing else touches. It also helps with the cough.

TIM: You must have good parties.

RICHARD: Oh p-lease. It's not a party drug. It's hideous. It tastes revolting and cuts you out of the world. I have mean dreams.

TIM: Like what?

RICHARD: I have a recurring one. My boat has broken down in the Congo but everyone else gets a nice little boat ride. I have to walk through this jungle with snakes and spiders and quicksand. When I fall into it someone pulls me out but I always sink back in. People drop supplies from a helicopter but it can't land. I'm angry and lonely. But I learn a lot. I see a gorilla having a baby. Everyone has seen a gorilla in a book but the actual experience is something else.

TIM: Thank you. There's a question…

RICHARD: Space shuttle crashed this morning.

TIM: I saw that.

RICHARD: Schoolteacher died in it.

TIM: That's right. There's a question we're asking everyone we interview. Is there a message about living with AIDS that you want the world to know?

RICHARD: I don't think I'll get to see your play.

> TIM *rubs* RICHARD*'s knee.*

♦ ♦ ♦ ♦ ♦

Albion Street Clinic waiting room.

Enter two DOCTORS.

DOCTOR 1: John 2118.

DOCTOR 2: Tim 2117.

> TIM *and* JOHN *go to separate consulting rooms. Their* DOCTORS *speak in unison.* TIM *and* JOHN *respond simultaneously.*

DOCTORS 1 and 2: How do you define your sexuality: homosexual, bisexual, transsexual?

JOHN: Homosexual.   TIM: Homo.

DOCTORS 1 and 2: Do you practice anal sex?

JOHN: Yes.   TIM: Practice makes perfect.

DOCTORS 1 and 2: Okay and are you active or passive?

JOHN: Well, both.   TIM: Kinda, both.

DOCTORS 1 and 2: If versatile, what ratio?

JOHN: Oh… Well… Fifty-fifty.   TIM: Twenty-eighty. Pitching. Ah,
                                    dicking. Mostly a top.

DOCTORS 1 and 2: Are you in a relationship?

JOHN: Yes.   TIM: Yes.

DOCTORS 1 and 2: Would you say it was monogamous?

JOHN: Yes.   TIM: Um, well, no.

DOCTORS 1 and 2: How many women have you slept with in the last six
    months?

JOHN: None.   TIM: None.

DOCTORS 1 and 2: How many men?

JOHN: One.   TIM: Some; three; eight—Eight.

DOCTORS 1 and 2: Have you paid for sex in the past month?

JOHN: No. I haven't.   TIM: Ken's. Not much. Never
                                    prostitutes. That's what you
                                    mean?

The DOCTORS *scrawl notes.*

DOCTORS 1 and 2: Okay. I need to also ask you how you would feel in
    two weeks if I told you that you were positive.

JOHN: I would be devastated.   TIM: I'm involved in a theatre project
                                    about AIDS, so I know it's not a
                                    death sentence.

DOCTORS 1 and 2: What support mechanisms do you have?

JOHN: My boyfriend.   TIM: My boyfriend.

DOCTOR 2: [*to* TIM] Your glands were up all over your body. I'll take
    some blood now.

Albion Street. TIM *and* JOHN *are leaving the clinic.*

JOHN: [*to* TIM] Probably just the flu. Mine weren't up.

TIM: Yeah. I'm not bothered. See that construction worker guy with the
    beer belly? What's he doing in there?

JOHN: Cruising. Should we walk to Oxford Street for lunch?

There's a bounce in TIM*'s step.*

TIM: Sure.

JOHN: Not like that.

TIM: What? Shut up. I just had an AIDS test. I'm a fast-lane gay now.

He moves as a fast-lane gay moves.

JOHN: I think you might need a biscuit after the blood test.

TIM: What'd he say: two weeks we have to wait for the result?

Albion Street Clinic waiting room. DOCTOR 2 *approaches* TIM *and* JOHN.

DOCTOR 2: Tim 2117.

TIM *leaps forward.*

TIM: My turn. Thanks for ruining the surprise, Negative Nancy.

JOHN: Ask her what caused the glands thing.

A consulting room. DOCTOR 2 *takes a seat.*

DOCTOR 2: Thanks. Take a seat, Tim. Tim, I'm sorry to inform you that you are positive.

TIM: Shit, you're kidding.

DOCTOR 2: This is the result sheet.

TIM: It's not that I don't believe you, but my boyfriend was just told he's negative.

DOCTOR 2: Right. And obviously you have a sexual relationship with him?

TIM: For like nine years.

DOCTOR 2: Okay. Well… I'll just ask you to return outside. I'll just need a moment.

The waiting room. TIM *approaches* JOHN. *The* DOCTOR *yells, unvoiced.*

JOHN: Tim?

TIM: John.

JOHN: Tim.

TIM: John…

JOHN: What?

TIM: I'm positive.

JOHN*'s brow furrows.*

JOHN: But I'm negative.

TIM: The doctors are yelling. Why? They're yelling.

JOHN *shrugs.* TIM *puts his arm around* JOHN. DOCTOR 2
approaches.

DOCTOR 2: Tim and John would you both like to come in, please…

A consulting room. Instantaneous.

…Thank you. John. I'm sorry. You have been given the wrong
result.

TIM: No.

DOCTOR 2: You are in fact positive, John. I'm terribly sorry. I should
explain. If your result is negative you see a counsellor, and if you
are positive you see a doctor. The clerk put your file in the wrong
pigeonhole and the counsellor gave you the result without checking
it. I am terribly sorry. This should not happen. I am truly so sorry. I
want to take some blood from both of you and do a cell count. John,
if you would like to come lie on the bed.

◆ ◆ ◆ ◆ ◆

At home.

TIM *and* JOHN *are in bed.*

JOHN: How long have we been trying to get to sleep?

TIM: I drifted off before.

JOHN: I have no idea what time it is.

TIM *lifts up* JOHN*'s shirt with his mouth. He snakes his head
under* JOHN*'s shirt.*

TIM: I know you hate it when I do this. I love it. It's so warm. Is it
Tuesday or Monday?

JOHN: Dunno. Don't care. Can you not stretch my T-shirt?

TIM: I'm not. I can hear the little meteorites in your tummy.

JOHN: What does this mean for my business? We've just signed the
papers.

TIM: Nothing. It means nothing. You still practise.

JOHN: I tell Craig.

TIM: Confidentially. Tell your business partner. But let's limit who we
tell. A gay actor's enough, let alone an infected poofter looking to
be cast. Maybe I thought doing a play about HIV made me immune.
Soft Targets isn't going great and they want to perform it in the

Mardi Gras Festival but I'll be touring *Brighton Beach Memoirs* then. Maybe they don't want me in it. They love butcher's paper too much. When that Challenger thing crashed, the NASA thing, the actors all came running in with an idea and they want to start the play set in space with spacemen hoovering the set—and I don't know if that's good. The play might be a disaster.

JOHN: Do you think I infected you?

> TIM *doesn't answer.*

The way our cells are, me being more advanced, you with your high T8s…

TIM: It's not important.

JOHN: I just wish I hadn't infected you.

> TIM *comes out from under the T-shirt.*

TIM: We don't know if that's what happened. We can never know. It didn't even have a name. Didn't know it was lurking.

JOHN: But from who? I've had sex with two other people. Peter's negative. How unlucky can I be?

TIM: Doctors don't know enough about this yet. We're both infected. That's all we know. I have a surprise. Condoms and lube. We are going to welcome them into our family.

JOHN: I don't want to have anal sex, Tim. That's how we got into this mess.

TIM: John. Come on. Sex isn't a sin. It's ours.

JOHN: I don't want to have sex.

TIM: Okay.

> TIM *puts his hand on* JOHN's *chest.* JOHN *responds automatically, rub rub rub, pat pat pat, kiss.*

I'm going to leave *Soft Targets.*

JOHN: Don't.

TIM: It's too much with *Brighton* performances at night and workshops in the day. It was my project. I started it. I was curious. The baby's been ripped from my arms and it has a dimension to it now that's… It's taking its toll. *Brighton*'s going to tour. I have to consider my health now.

JOHN: Are we eighty?

TIM: I'm going to tell Peter Kingston at Griffin. We are eighty. All of a sudden… It's hit me now.

JOHN: We're twenty-five.

TIM: I think it's hit me now.

JOHN: Let's try to sleep.

TIM: I don't want to sleep. I want to stay awake for the rest of my life. I want you to hold me. I want my mum to scoop me up and my schoolteachers and all my friends and family… I want everyone to hold me and say it's all right.

JOHN: It's all right, Tim.

   JOHN *touches* TIM: *rub rub rub, pat pat pat, kiss.*

TIM: But it's not. We are going to die.

◆ ◆ ◆ ◆ ◆

TIM*'s childhood bedroom:* TIM *is half dressed in a late eighties suit. His mother is taking up the hem. It is 1990.*

MARY-GERT: I'll kill your father for eating the glacé cherries. Hold still, please, Tim.

TIM: [*the trouser leg*] Leave it to bag.

MARY-GERT: Did you see the letters for you? Must update your address, dear. Haven't lived here for ten years.

TIM: They weren't important.

MARY-GERT: I didn't know your brother was so much taller. You don't wear a suit at work, I suppose, if it's phone work.

TIM: That was volunteer. I'm paid to be face-to-face now. I'm like a social worker.

MARY-GERT: And an actor.

TIM: Yeah.

MARY-GERT: We haven't seen a play since, I dunno, five years, *Brighton Beach Memoirs* and I worry about you paying your bills…

TIM: I had three solid years after graduating but I'm not Mel Gibson or Judy Davis.

MARY-GERT: Wish I'd been an actor.

TIM: I'm writing a play about a guy on day release from prison. I've applied for a grant to develop it.

MARY-GERT: I remember you in *Romeo and Juliet.* You were so— beautiful.

TIM: Mmmh, I didn't train to be Cop Number Two on *Australia's Most Wanted.* Last couple of years I've been turning down acting gigs—

working at ACON has become a very important place in my life, Mum. We're seeing a lot more boys from other agencies, like STD clinics or the AIDS Bus that works up at The Wall. That's where boy sex-workers find their customers.

MARY-GERT: Oh God. I have to hide the choc-drops from your father and now I'll have to hide cake ingredients too. I'll buy glacé cherries in the morning, I suppose. Is John eating here?

TIM: No. At his.

MARY-GERT: I set up the sunroom. If he wants to stay.

TIM: Thank you. Does Anna's fiancé stay in the sunroom?

MARY-GERT: He doesn't stay. Maybe John could pick up some glacé cherries on his way over.

TIM: No. He's had a rough day.

MARY-GERT: He wouldn't mind. Surely. You could call him there. [*The hem*] Oh blow, I've done that wrong. I'll repin it.

MARY-GERT *repins the hem.*

TIM: John was having a big thing with his folks. Send Dad or I'll go.

MARY-GERT: I wouldn't want to trouble anyone; only people are coming round the next day—people from out of town.

TIM: How many functions are we having?

MARY-GERT: Just the normal amount, Tim. She is our only daughter.

Enter DICK.

DICK: Who's our only daughter?

MARY-GERT: Anna, Dick. Ask a silly question…

DICK: How's the suit? Oh yeah. Not bad.

MARY-GERT: Smart.

DICK: Bit of room.

MARY-GERT: No.

DICK: You've lost weight.

TIM: I go to the gym.

DICK: The gym? Well. You box?

TIM: No. Weights.

DICK: Good.

TIM: You ate the glacé cherries.

DICK: Yes.

MARY-GERT: Yes. And I'm dark.

DICK: I'll buy more. You get the letters we kept for you?

TIM: Yeah.

DICK: Should update your address, mate.

TIM: I have. They're ancient.

DICK: So you, ah, hear we're going to have a spit at the reception?

TIM: Nice.

DICK: In a ballroom.

TIM: Mum said.

DICK: Yeah, over at Ripponlea. No, it'll be a big show, don't you worry.

TIM: So it'll be the full deal? The mass and all?

DICK: Yeah. Course.

TIM: Communion and all?

DICK: Yes.

TIM: Is she a Catholic still?

MARY-GERT: Tim.

DICK: And we got an orchestra.

TIM: Jesus.

MARY-GERT: Tim.

DICK: A small chamber orchestra…

TIM: Bit over the top, isn't it?

MARY-GERT: Tim.

DICK: She's my only daughter.

TIM: The best wedding I ever saw was my friend Morna's. It was a simple exchange of vows in a room full of friends. It was very moving.

DICK: But this is what your sister wants.

TIM: I think it sounds tasteless.

MARY-GERT: Tim.

DICK: Cool it.

TIM: No. This feels like a charade.

DICK: I won't have you destroy this wedding.

MARY-GERT: It's all right, Dick.

TIM: I'm being a jerk. I'm sorry. I'm in a strange…

DICK: If you don't want to be involved then don't be.

> DICK *exits*.

MARY-GERT: Thank you, Timothy. Slip them off, please.

> TIM *takes off the pants*.

Gently. I've pinned that, please.

TIM: Sorry.

MARY-GERT: Bite your tongue. I've got relatives arriving from everywhere this week. I don't need stirring.

TIM: I'm not stirring.

> TIM *has stuck himself in the calf with a pin from the hem.*

MARY-GERT: Careful. You stuck yourself.

TIM: It's tiny.

MARY-GERT: Needs Mercurochrome.

TIM: No need and you should use Betadine now.

> *Enter* JOHN.

JOHN: Hello.

TIM: [*to* JOHN] Topolino [*a nickname*].

MARY-GERT: Hello John, you look sick.

JOHN: No.

MARY-GERT: You're all right?

JOHN: A cold.

MARY-GERT: He doesn't look well.

TIM: He's fine, Mum. Don't fuss.

JOHN: Just had a long day.

MARY-GERT: It's a farce here tonight but you're welcome to join us for dinner. Better get going on it. Heavens, look at the time.

> MARY-GERT *exits.* JOHN *has a tickle in his throat.*

TIM: It went okay?

JOHN: Yeah.

TIM: What'd they say?

JOHN: Well. Went pretty good. Dad'd already suspected something. He found it strange that we went to Europe five months after I opened the practice. And with selling my half. That'd never not ring alarm bells. So…

TIM: Probably relieved you're not pregnant.

JOHN: They asked about my disability insurance of course. Mum was concerned about my weight and just kept blowing her nose.

TIM: My dad was asking about me losing weight.

JOHN: You haven't.

TIM: Have. At the gym.

JOHN: Oh, yeah. I think Mum wanted to cry, but she wasn't going to in front of anyone else. It might be better I leave them alone tonight. To talk and all.

TIM: Slumber party? Gert set up the sunroom—of course.

JOHN: Cool.

TIM: Could sneak back in here later like old times.

JOHN *coughs*.

Bloody sunroom. You're not my girlfriend home from the social. Reckon Mum'd beg Phoebe to share a bed with me now. I'm still in grade nine but Anna gets trumpeters and a banquet.

JOHN: What's your gripe with Anna?

TIM: I think I need to tell them.

JOHN: About what?

TIM: About my status.

JOHN: Tim. You can't.

TIM: Why?

JOHN: The wedding. You can't do it the week of Anna's wedding.

TIM: I know that. I know. But it's coming. And how much preparation can I do? I can't read every book and ask every counsellor. I'm just nervous about the wedding: being in front of all those people. And today I read... I read something today...

JOHN: Where?

TIM: I'm reading that book is all. It's actually called *Telling Your Parents You Have HIV*.

JOHN: I am reeling from Mum and Dad, Tim. Please don't be selfish.

TIM: What?

JOHN: When the time's right. This isn't just a single conversation. This isn't one piece of info. This is telling them everything. They'll want to know everything. What, are you going to paint a picture of your seizure—tell them you were on the floor of the toilet—in a puddle of piss and shit, looking over your shoulder and twitching? You going to give them that image to take into Anna's wedding?

TIM: I'm not going to do it the week of the wedding.

JOHN: Or the week that I tell mine.

TIM: My ears are burning. Your parents are at home saying I infected you and...

JOHN: There was no discussion about who infected who.

TIM: Cell counts can be wrong. I know you don't believe it. I know you blame me.

JOHN: Don't tell me what I know.

TIM: What if there was a way to determine who infected who? You'd want to know, John.

JOHN: I don't want you to undermine my positive thinking.

TIM: Err, that's from that play.

JOHN: What?

TIM: That Alex Harding play we saw.

JOHN: I liked that play. They didn't believe they were going to die from this.

TIM: Do you?

JOHN: No, I don't.

TIM: Is that why we haven't made a will?

JOHN: Maybe we should. [*He coughs.*]

TIM: One problem is, I've got nothing to leave you. Want some old acting books? Actually, they'll go to Phoebe. You can have my clothes but most of them are yours. It's shit. And anything I treasure was a gift from you anyway.

    Enter MARY-GERT.

Hey Mum…

MARY-GERT: There's the Mercurochrome for your leg.

TIM: Thanks. It's tiny. [*To* JOHN] You do it, John.

MARY-GERT: I'm glad you opened your letters.

TIM: Just leave them. I read them. [*To* JOHN] On my calf. It's dried up anyway.

    JOHN *puts the antiseptic ointment on* TIM.

JOHN: I'll draw a smiley face.

MARY-GERT: I put them in your book on your bag.

    Silence.

TIM: I am reading that for my work…

MARY-GERT: I know… I assumed that…

    Silence. JOHN *is alive to the change in* TIM *and* MARY-GERT.

TIM: I should help you with your platters.

MARY-GERT: Yes. Flat out…

TIM: I like the smoked salmon one best.

MARY-GERT: Yes.

TIM: Could I have lunch with you and Dad tomorrow?

MARY-GERT: We'll all have lunch at some stage.

TIM: No. Just the three of us.

JOHN: Tim.

MARY-GERT: [*calling out*] Dick!

TIM: No, don't get him.

MARY-GERT: Tell me everything's all right.

JOHN: Tim.

TIM: No, it's okay…

   Enter DICK.

MARY-GERT: Tim wants to talk about something.

DICK: Go on then…

TIM: No, not now. Tomorrow. We'll have lunch.

DICK: You'll make madam fret. Tell us now, Tim.

TIM: I'll discuss it tomorrow.

DICK: No. Go on. Tell us.

TIM: Well, come sit down.

JOHN: Tim.

TIM: Do you want to stay?

JOHN: You grab me if you want me.

   JOHN *exits*.

TIM: Come sit, Mum. There's something I've wanted to tell you for some time but didn't think I could; I love you and I'm afraid I'm going to hurt you.

   Silence.

John and I have HIV, the virus that causes AIDS.

   Silence.

MARY-GERT: What a waste. All that talent.

TIM: I'm not dead yet.

DICK: How long have you boys known?

TIM: We were tested five years ago. That's when we were tested.

DICK: And how is your health?

TIM: Mine's pretty good but John's is failing. He's already had pneumonia.

MARY-GERT: That beautiful boy. I knew something was up. He doesn't look well. I said that.

DICK: What does it mean? Do you have AIDS?

TIM: No. I have HIV. It's the immunodeficiency retrovirus that can cause AIDS. I think, I think it would be a good idea... They have counsellors at ACON—where I work.

DICK: This is a terrible blow.

MARY-GERT: I knew there was something because you were spending so much money on travel. Italy and then Bali. We didn't even get to see photos of Italy.

TIM: We stopped taking them. I have one. John with this disgusting sore on his face standing in front of Michelangelo's *Pietà*. He got a fever. We barely saw Florence. We came home early. And Bali was... I had Bali-belly before we left Sydney. We have been fairly sick. I'm okay at the moment. But I have had some dodgy times and that's why you should know and I could book you in to see a counsellor. I think it would be good. Professional support.

MARY-GERT: But I don't understand how you got it? If it's just you and John...

TIM: We both have it.

> *Slight pause.*

DICK: Yes.

TIM: John has had to leave his clinic.

MARY-GERT: God help us.

TIM: He was too sick to cope and he was finding it hard to deal with patients' questions. It wasn't a choice in the end. My T8 count, the suppressor cells, are at a good stage and my other cells are basically good. And my T4 cells are in a normal range.

MARY-GERT: We don't know what any of that means.

TIM: T4s are the cells that the virus destroys so they are the ones they monitor. I am just telling you everything so that you can get more information... [*Unheard by* MARY-GERT] Dad?

> DICK *is bright.*

DICK: [*unheard by* MARY-GERT] Fish and chips for tea.

TIM: [*unheard by* MARY-GERT] Dad?

> DICK *is firm.*

DICK: [*unheard by* MARY-GERT] I voted for Whitlam in '72.

TIM: [*unheard by* MARY-GERT] Dad?

> DICK *explodes with grief.*

DICK: [*unheard by* MARY-GERT] Please don't do this to us.

    DICK *is composed.*

MARY-GERT: Dick?

DICK: [*to* MARY-GERT] I am going to go for a drive. Think I might.

MARY-GERT: Oh. You sure, dear?

DICK: I think I want to. I'll buy the cherries.

MARY-GERT: Okay, dear.

    DICK *pats* TIM *and exits.*

I think you'll be comfortable in here. I put an extra blanket on.

TIM: I think you should see the counsellor. ACON have an office like mine in Melbourne.

MARY-GERT: Okay, Tim.

TIM: Dad won't.

MARY-GERT: No. Probably he'll decline.

TIM: That's okay.

MARY-GERT: I should sew this hem. So much to do. Anna's got dinner underway. A difficult week.

TIM: I don't want to sabotage the wedding but I am dreading people saying that John's not well and speculating and...

MARY-GERT: In a way it's good the wedding's coming up because I have something to concentrate on.

TIM: And I opened those letters this morning. I read the letters you bought me and...

MARY-GERT: Good.

TIM: No. A few were from the Red Cross and I thought: maybe a blood donation request...

MARY-GERT: Yes. Well. I guess you can't. I knew from the start that nothing good could come of this but you can't intervene.

TIM: Mum. No. The letters were chasing me up... I made a blood donation in June 1981. It was pooled with nineteen others. I'm one of the last to be contacted. The patient who received the blood has developed AIDS and I might have given it to this poor person. I had a strange viral thing back in '81. I think that may have been my seroconversion.

MARY-GERT: What does this mean?

TIM: I've had it for nine years not five, Mum. So I had to tell you.

MARY-GERT: I see.

TIM: And it means I probably infected John.

MARY-GERT: I see.

TIM: They want a written response. I'll write to the blood bank and tell them everything—that I was tested positive in '85.

MARY-GERT: And that you didn't know. How could you know? Nobody knew then.

TIM: I can't tell John now. I don't want to share this letter with him, tonight. I hate the speculation and the not knowing, Mum. I was comfortable with the thought John had infected me, but it's awful to think I may have infected him. As though I've killed the man I love. [*Aside*] I never wrote the letter to the Red Cross.

On stage, The Stables Theatre, Darlinghurst, Sydney, 1991.

Actors GIA CARIDES, DAVID FIELD, VALERIE BADER, YVES STENING, BEN FRANKLIN *and director* PETER KINGSTON *sit in a circle of mismatched chairs. One spare chair is for* TIM *but strangely it is a wheelchair.*

KINGSTON: Tim! Here he is: the writer of *Thieving Boy* himself.

TIM: Hello. Sorry I'm late, everyone. I've had this lurgy. And I woke up with a fever and could barely get up. Sorry.

KINGSTON: Hope you're better.

TIM: Keep your distance.

KINGSTON: Now you don't know Ben Franklin.

TIM: Kind of. Yep, g'day.

BEN: G'day Tim.

KINGSTON: Gia Carides, David Field, Valerie Bader and Yves Stening.

   Hellos.

Well, we were just talking generally about the play and your wonderful changes. Sit there, Tim.

TIM: [*the wheelchair*] In that?

KINGSTON: Sure. Gia, you said…

GIA: Me? Oh, just about the central question really. About whether it is 'family as prison' in a way…

VALERIE: …And if this is a world you really know about.

   TIM'*s chair is unstable.*

TIM: Sorry, is my chair rolling?

KINGSTON: You right, Tim?

TIM: Yeah.

DAVID: It was unclear to me whether you'd moved your bowels today? I couldn't tell really.

TIM: Pardon? My chair's rolling.

VALERIE: Your haemoglobin is still good. Very good.

TIM: [*the wheelchair*] Are there brakes?

KINGSTON: [*the workshop*] At eleven. You right?

YVES: Your T-cell count reads as 370.

TIM: Why has it been cut? Where's John?

VALERIE: He's gone, mate. You okay?

KINGSTON: We'll stage a public reading.

TIM: Am I late?

DAVID: Nurse?!

TIM: Fuck. John's hurt. He's broken his leg on the top oval playing footy. His mum and dad and Father Wallbridge are at the hospital now turning off the life-support machine. Dreamer. I'm too hot. No more warm-ups. Excuse me, I'm in the middle of a workshop of a play, my play, I wrote it and tomorrow is the last day's rehearsal yesterday or a decade ago.

DAVID: You have some leukoplakia on the side of your tongue.

GIA: We think it is Epstein-Barr virus; we're having the dramaturg look at it.

BEN: When it presents as oral hairy leukoplakia it's considered an AIDS-defining illness.

TIM: Exposition to heal before opening—did he say AIDS? Right, it's AIDS, everyone. Big thought. The sleep of the dead and fuck, it's thirty-nine-point-four degrees celsius o'clock and when's Monday? If you feel right by then, I'll be happy for you to go. Oh, thank you. 'Can you stick your hands in your head? Oh no.'

GIA: The critic who did your bronchoscopy said he saw cysts that are consistent with PCP.

KINGSTON: I think we should start with a fantastic…

VALERIE: …course of Pentamidine.

BEN: It's fairly toxic.

YVES: How am I meant to piss in this thing? Nurse.

TIM *tries to dress into a suit and tie.*

TIM: Comb my hair shave suit spew in the sink and one small step dizzy nurse buzz fuck it. I don't think I can go. Knowing my luck I'd vomit in the foyer.

KINGSTON: Will you make it to the reading? Your public awaits.

TIM: I can't do it, Peter Kingston. I'm not going in a wheelchair and, these monsters, under my bed, they'll drink my blood if I step into an operating theatre venue so I can't go I'm afraid. I'm so afraid. Peter Kingston, I have AIDS. Do people know that, should I make it clearer, for the audience, my friends, that are here tonight, that'll be there tonight, at the theatre, should I tell them, what should I tell them?

GIA: AIDS fucker faggot.

KINGSTON: That you have really bad gastro.

BEN: That you're dead and died long ago.

DAVID: Oh no. Nurse.

An answering machine beeps.

GIA: It's Gia. They pissed themselves, Tim.

An answering machine beeps.

VOICE: Tim, it's Libby. *Thieving Boy* was great, I nearly wet myself. Hope you get a production and that your gastro gets better.

An answering machine beeps.

VOICE: It's Craig. Hope your gastro is getting better. I loved your play. It deserves a production, call me.

An answering machine beeps.

VOICE: James here, Tim. I told Morna you were in hospital. I assumed she already knew. Sorry. Call me.

An answering machine beeps.

VOICE: Tim. Darling, how are you? You're in hospital? Why didn't you tell us? Is everything okay? Sorry to ask, but everyone is wondering if you have AIDS.

The answering machine beep becomes a life-support machine.

VOICES: [*simultaneous*] Hi Tim, I've just heard that you are in hospital and that you have AIDS. Is that true? I don't want you and John to die. I'm scared.

[*Simultaneous*] I've just heard you guys are not well, that you have AIDS. I'm really sorry to hear it. You guys are both the ones I'd least expected to get it. How sick are you?

[*Simultaneous*] You poor bastards. You poor bastards. Oh God. You poor bastards. You poor poor bastards. Oh God.

TIM: I'm fine.

> *Recorded audience laughter.*

I'll be back at work in a couple of days.

> *Recorded audience laughter.* TIM *strains to hear where it is coming from.*

But I'm not as weak as you think.

> *Recorded audience laughter.* PETER KINGSTON *has a cassette tape for* TIM.

KINGSTON: The cast taped the reading for you. It's hard to hear but I guess you know all the lines.

> *Recorded audience laughter.*

TIM: They're laughing. I made people laugh.

> Thieving Boy *recording fades.*

♦ ♦ ♦ ♦ ♦

The Hotel Ramada Renaissance, Circular Quay, Sydney.

MAIDS *prepare the bed with hotel linen and drag on* TIM *and* JOHN*'s luggage—complete with hotel tags.* TIM *and* JOHN *are in their Sunday best.*

JOHN: Check out the bed. 'Sticky long goes for the mark!'

> JOHN *dives onto the bed. He is slow and stiff.*

Ow.

TIM: You right?

JOHN: Don't laugh.

TIM: Can I have a ciggie?

JOHN: No.

TIM: On the balcony? Please? You can see the Opera House. Let me have a ciggie.

JOHN: No.

TIM: Why?

JOHN: Um, because you've had pneumonia.

TIM: Oh, who hasn't?

JOHN: Don't you want to get well?

TIM: Shoosh. We're treating ourselves this weekend.

JOHN: You eat McDonald's and Tim Tams behind my back and it stresses me.

> TIM *jumps on the bed.*

TIM: [*as a public announcement*] All kids, please report to the giggle factory, all kids.

JOHN: No shoes on the bed.

TIM: Oh, Jesus fuck; what's up with all the rules?

> *Brief tense silence. Enter an extremely sexy* WAITER. *He is wearing the shirt, vest, badge and complete uniform you'd expect of a hotel employee but for blue board shorts instead of trousers. This draws no comment or query. In fact, it is only* TIM *that can see it.*

WAITER: Room service.

> TIM *rushes to avoid being caught jumping on the bed.*

TIM: Come in if you're beautiful. [*To himself, on seeing the* WAITER] Ooh shit.

WAITER: Good evening.

> *The* WAITER *wheels in a trolley and sets a small table. The trolley contains two covered meals and the complete table setting.*

TIM: [*to* WAITER] Hi. [*To* JOHN] Mr Caleo, will you join me?

JOHN: Thank you.

TIM: Champagne for Mr Caleo, please.

JOHN: Can't.

TIM: Can.

JOHN: Can't. My stomach. I can't.

TIM: [*to the* WAITER] Drown it with gravy. Just leave the boat.

WAITER: Very good.

TIM: Have you worked here long?

WAITER: Two years.

TIM: Must have been at school when you started.

WAITER: Still at school.
TIM: Oh.

The WAITER *has efficiently set the table.*

WAITER: Will there be anything else, sir?
TIM: Um. No. Oh…

TIM *hands the* WAITER *a tip.*

WAITER: Thank you, sir.
TIM: Bye…

The WAITER *exits.* JOHN *clears his throat.*

JOHN: Did you give him twenty?
TIM: Yeah.
JOHN: That's too much.
TIM: Well?
JOHN: Well, I already felt bad about spending all this money on staying here and you bought a new tie and it worries me. You are making my ulcer worse.

TIM *pours champagne for* JOHN. JOHN *frowns.*

TIM: We just need some glamour. That's all. More champagne?
JOHN: My stomach'll kill.

They start to eat.

Sorry. We'll have a nice time tonight.

Silence. They eat.

Six months is nothing.
TIM: Pardon?
JOHN: It's November.
TIM: I know.
JOHN: I was side-swiped when the doctor said 'lymphoma'. I heard it before he said it. 'Aggressive' and that survival is unlikely. He was talking and I could just hear bits but I heard each word before he said it, was what it was like.
TIM: I'm really scared. I don't want you to die.
JOHN: I don't either.
TIM: Have you come to any decision about treatment?

Silence again.

You have a couple of days. He said to think it over.

Silence. They eat.

You could call Peter in Melbourne. He's known you so long... He's a nurse in this field even and he knows what chemo will do and what it means if it is disseminated.

JOHN: I'm going to call the doctor on Monday and you know, they'll, they said, um, they'll start straight away. So that's the way it's going. I just made the decision. I'm taking the ten per cent chance of chemo. I like that number more than comfort.

TIM: You say it like I should know.

JOHN: I'm not going to give up without a fight.

TIM: You're not doing this for me, are you? I mean, are you just trying to stay alive for me?

JOHN: Don't be ridiculous, I'm just doing it for me.

They eat another morsel.

TIM: A toast. To your decision.

JOHN: To the obvious choice.

TIM: I wish there were others.

They drink.

I spoke to Peter. I called him.

JOHN: You never call Peter.

TIM: He said he could take some leave to help us later in the year.

JOHN: We'll see.

Silence. They eat.

I wish I'd got to play for Essendon.

TIM: Yeah. I wish that too. Will chemo make your eyelashes fall out?

JOHN: I don't know. AZT made them grow longer.

TIM: Really?

JOHN: Think so.

Silence. They eat.

I wish I'd been a chiropractor for longer.

TIM: You started your own practice. No regrets there.

JOHN: No. Sure.

TIM: I'm sad my acting career didn't take off.

JOHN: You did all right. I'm sorry I never got to have sex with a woman. There's no way I could now.

TIM: I wanted to have kids with Phoebe. Probably a turkey baster but maybe we'd root. Scared I'll get duped on legacy.

JOHN: No one to look after us when we're old?

TIM: Something like that. I regret not knowing what breeder-sex is like.

JOHN: Me too.

TIM: So like, do you really desire to?

JOHN: I'm curious.

TIM: What if you decided you liked it better than with me?

JOHN: Not a possibility. You're too cute.

Silence. They eat.

TIM: John, there's something I want to tell you. I played around a bit when you were away last year.

Silence. JOHN *clears his throat.*

I'm sorry.

JOHN: I thought with this AIDS stuff that would have stopped.

TIM: I'm sorry.

JOHN: Why do you do this to me? Was it anyone I know?

TIM: Well, no. No.

JOHN: Who?

TIM: Couple of guys in the sauna.

JOHN: I feel like that's not the truth.

TIM: No.

JOHN: It hurts.

Silence. They eat.

TIM: That's my biggest regret. All the times I hurt you.

JOHN: Mmmh. Don't want to talk about that.

TIM: No.

They eat. JOHN *can't look at* TIM *so he looks to the floor. He notices something on the bags and investigates.*

JOHN: They've labelled our luggage 'Mr and Mrs Conigrave'.

TIM: No? Show me.

JOHN: I'm keeping this label.

TIM: [*unheard by* JOHN] You were yourself again in an instant. You were yourself again as you had been after every other time I'd hurt you.

TIM *stands and raises his glass.*

[*To* JOHN] To my darling John, for the years of love, comfort and support.

JOHN *raises his glass.*

JOHN: Thanks for being my boyfriend.

TIM: Cheers, mate. To all the times you let me fall asleep in front of the TV with my head in your lap. All the times we laughed.

JOHN: No wuckers. Thanks for the holidays. Europe and everything. And thank you for being here now.

TIM: It's been fun.

TIM *leans across and kisses* JOHN *but puts his elbow in the gravy.*

Fuck.

JOHN: Such a dag.

TIM: [*unheard by* JOHN] After dinner we lay down on the bed and cuddled.

They move to the bed.

Just holding each other. You are here in my arms. But the sorrow rose up again.

◆ ◆ ◆ ◆ ◆

Sacred Heart Hospice, Darlinghurst, Sydney.

ORDERLIES *strip the bed.* JOHN *sleeps. They become surrounded by 'Get Well' cards.*

Enter PHOEBE *holding a tray of three takeaway coffees. It is still 1991.*

PHOEBE: He's asleep.

TIM: Phoebe, come over.

PHOEBE: Coffees from Café Hernandez; best in Sydney apparently.

TIM: Look how cute John's ears are.

PHOEBE: Given us a fright the two of you being in here together.

TIM: He's on an opiate cloud floating somewhere.

PHOEBE: You drifted away for a few days.

TIM: Fuck, nice coffee.

PHOEBE: Thought you wouldn't be the same. You know you told your
　　mother to stop having affairs?

TIM: I know. I heard.

PHOEBE: I bought grapes too.

TIM: Everyone does.

PHOEBE: They were in the foyer.

TIM: Thank you. I love them. And a shoulder rub. Everyone offers a
　　shoulder rub.

PHOEBE: Would you like one?

TIM: Would love one.

PHOEBE: How are you?

TIM: Great. There are eight people running errands for John and me at
　　the moment. Eight.

PHOEBE: Great.

TIM: It is great. Well, we're waiting to hear more about John. The
　　lymphoma. He had six months and… Well. Still, life's okay but I
　　don't know if I believe in an afterlife.

PHOEBE: Have some grapes.

TIM: Thank you. What if John's soul is just reabsorbed into the greater
　　power of the universe?

PHOEBE: I don't know. [*The grapes*] They're Thompson seedless.

TIM: I don't want him to become blended energy. I want him to be there
　　waiting for me. Are grapes even in season?

PHOEBE: Yes. Relax, you're knotty.

　　　TIM *strokes* JOHN*'s face and wipes his brow.*

TIM: My chiropractor's getting lazy. Look at him, so innocent, serene.

　　　TIM *seems to be still stroking* JOHN*'s face or wiping his brow but
　　　in fact he is darkening under his eyes with stage make-up and
　　　taking the youthful colour from his skin.*

PHOEBE: I'll leave the grapes here.

TIM: [*to* PHOEBE] I've been in the forest of madness, Phoebe. They
　　tried to get his lung fixed; stabbed little John with a spear, pouring
　　chemical irritants into him to try and make his popped lung heal:
　　hurting him to make him scar back together, and they hooked him up
　　to suction and this drain with this little bottle and, night after night,
　　we'd be watching *Home and Away*, hoping the bubbles wouldn't
　　come—meaning it hadn't stuck—but they did come—always, no

not always, twice, it happened twice watching *Home and Away*—meaning they'd have to pour more of this cruel shit into him—and my head was pounding and I couldn't bear to keep on going to all the attempts to fix him, but I did go, but one night his cough made me sleep on the couch and he was so let down in the morning but I had to do it. He's had so much pain. In my sick fantasies I say walk to the light. It took some heavy stuff to touch my headaches but I so knew I had them, the toxo lesions on my brain. I had to beg for a scan.

PHOEBE: I think this illness is unbelievable. It attacks a footballer's body and a writer's brain.

TIM: I'm an actor.

PHOEBE: Oh. Yeah.

TIM: You know what it's from? Toxoplasmosis?

PHOEBE: No.

TIM: Eating cat poo as a kid in the sandpit.

PHOEBE: Silly you, thinking that was a consequence-free environment.

TIM: That's right. I made that joke to Sam the doctor. He wears board shorts.

PHOEBE: Tim, if John goes, doesn't mean it's your turn…

TIM: I'm writing a new play.

PHOEBE: Excellent. Will the lesions get worse?

TIM: Everything does. My eye is fucking up, I think and… Actually, I should buzz to see when Doctor Sam's coming. There's a new thing on my eye.

TIM *buzzes for the doctor.*

Hey, check out our view. You can see The Wall. It's a good system; have unprotected sex and just cross the road.

PHOEBE: Convenient.

Enter a doctor named SAM *with a* SHRINK *called Dr Shepherd.*

SAM: Oh, he's asleep.

TIM: I just buzzed you. That only happens on hospital dramas. Were you waiting for your entrance?

SAM: Would have come before but we were following up something regarding John.

TIM: Sam? You know something. What is it?

SAM: Tim, John's scope was clear. There's no ulcer and no inflammation.

TIM: Meaning?

SAM: It's probably fair to say that his cancer is in remission.

TIM: Fuck…

SAM: This new regimen seems to be getting good results.

TIM: Fuck.

SAM: So we've just got to concentrate on fixing the lung. It's good news.

TIM: John won. Dr Sam, this is Phoebe.

SAM: Hello.

PHOEBE: Hello.

TIM: You did actually say 'remission'?

SAM: That's right. And the eye? You told…

TIM: Oh yeah, my peripheral vision's going, Sam. There's an extra coffee there…

SAM: I'm fine.   TIM: …If I'm not seeing double.

SAM: What have you noticed?

TIM: Yesterday Penny Cook was giving me a shoulder rub and she disappeared when I leant for the remote control.

SAM: You were watching the TV?

TIM: Was going to but Penny didn't want to. Then she disappeared.

PHOEBE: Penny is a friend of Tim's.

TIM: Yeah, Dr Ellie Fielding. I know her from Griffin.

SAM *examines* TIM*'s eyes with an ophthalmoscope.*

SAM: Pick a spot on the wall and keep focused on it.

TIM: John and I are cutting down. Turn away anyone in reception who looks B grade.

SAM: Just focus on the spot.

TIM: Head's in the way.

SAM: Hold still.

TIM: My God, John's ulcer. I should call Penny.

SAM: Yes. Extraordinary news. Just straight ahead.

TIM: Nice aftershave.

SAM: There seems to be a large white spot on your retina but it doesn't look like CMV. Shut your left eye and tell me when you can see my finger.

SAM *moves his index finger back and forth in front of* TIM*'s face.*

TIM: It goes there. It's back.

SAM: [*still examining*] Seems pretty large.

TIM: Phoebe was on *Prisoner*. Tell him.

PHOEBE: I was on *Prisoner*.

SHRINK: I thought you were familiar.

SAM: I suspect it's the lesion on your occipital lobe.

TIM: Brain damage? Permanent?

SAM: Well. Maybe, maybe not. As your toxo improves, we'll know. I'd
like you to speak to Dr Shepherd. She's a psychiatrist.

TIM: Why? I don't need to see a...

SAM: Tim, it's just... Sorry, Phoebe...

PHOEBE: Oh, of course. I'll go.

TIM: She should stay. She's a writer. If it comes out that I bonked my
mum I want her to put it in her memoirs.

PHOEBE: It's okay, Tim. I have to move the car.

TIM: Come back.

PHOEBE: I will.

> PHOEBE *exits.*

SAM: Tim, I want you to speak to Dr Shepherd because I think you're
hypermanic. You seem very up, very chatty, talking at a hundred
miles an hour.

TIM: I'm not up. I just feel good. John won. And this is the first time I
can be with my lover and not have to look after him.

SAM: Tim! It's important that we bring you down before you become
grandiose, thinking you're Jesus or spending all your money.

TIM: I won't. I'm completely B grade. I know that.

SAM: Yesterday a visitor told me you gave her a headache with all the
talk.

TIM: That was Gia Carides and she's the talker, not me.

SHRINK: [*to* TIM] Hello Tim. I just want to ask you some questions. [*To*
SAM] We'll have a chat, Sam.

TIM: Hi.

> SAM *exits.*

What are those tablets?

SHRINK: How do you feel today?

TIM: I feel very good.

SHRINK: How's being in here for you?

She scribbles notes about TIM*'s replies.*

TIM: Content. I'm enjoying myself. But for the hospital smells.

SHRINK: What sort of things have you been doing to occupy your
    time?

TIM: I'm writing a play.

SHRINK: A play? You feel creative?

TIM: Yes. It's called *Jimmy, an Angel, Stars and That* about a gay
    relationship where one partner is dying. I'm thinking of having a
    reading with some actor friends one day in the waiting room. You're
    welcome to come.

SHRINK: What else do you do to occupy yourself?

TIM: People visit. I hold court around John's bed, entertaining friends.

SHRINK: Okay.

TIM: I'm bright. Very happy. But that's good.

SHRINK: Okay. I'm going to put you on Haliperidol. You're manic
    because the cells in your brain have become hypersensitive to
    certain neurotransmitters. Haliperidol reduces the sensitivity. You
    can take this one now. You've had breakfast?

TIM: Yes. Do you think I am losing my mind?

SHRINK: I can't say dementia and memory loss won't happen.

TIM: Who would have thought, they have unhappy pills too?

SHRINK: They'll bring them with meals.

TIM: You're going to watch me take it.

SHRINK: Yes.

    TIM *takes the tablet. Enter* BOB CALEO.

TIM: And here's Bob. Well, works quick.

BOB: Hello Doctor, I'm Bob Caleo, John's father. Anything new?

TIM: No, Bob, she's *my* shrink. We got great news. Yuck. [*The pill*]
    Tastes gross.

    BOB *ignores* TIM.

SHRINK: I'll call on you in a week, Tim.

TIM: Take that coffee, Doctor. Have the spare coffee.

SHRINK: Oh. Thank you. We'll speak soon.

    The SHRINK *exits.*

TIM: Bye. Bob, good news.

BOB: Brought you this from the flat.

BOB *hands over some envelopes.* TIM *flicks through the envelopes.*

TIM: Oh thanks. Bills and stuff, hey? [*Aside*] I wonder what John would look like at that age? I reckon I could still love him even if he was an old wombat like Bob.

BOB: [*leaning over* JOHN] Hello John, it's Dad.

TIM: Bob, he's asleep.

BOB: Pardon?

TIM: I got good news. About John.

BOB: Well, I'm all ears.

JOHN: Dad?

BOB: Hello son. What have the doctors been saying?

JOHN: They just want [*cough*] keep trying to fix my lungs by [*cough*] antibiotics in them.

BOB: What...?   TIM: John, we got news.

BOB: ...I'm sorry, I can't hear him.

       JOHN *continues to cough.*

TIM: [*to* BOB] He can't speak loudly. It makes him cough. [*To* JOHN] Sam was here, John. The scope showed that the ulcer's gone. He said you're in remission. He's pretty sure. You beat it, John.

BOB: Remission? The cancer?

TIM: His cancer is in remission.

JOHN: Haven't you got [*cough*] hearing aid?

BOB: What did he...?

TIM: Asked if you've got your hearing aid.

BOB: [*to* TIM] I don't like wearing it. [*To* JOHN] The cancer, you've worked hard for it, son.

TIM: Here, Bob, have the seat. I'll sit on the bed.

JOHN: [*Cough*] all the cards will stop?

TIM: Don't strain yourself, John.

       BOB *strains to hear.*

He said the cards will stop.

BOB: He's hardly one hundred per cent.

JOHN: I only [*cough*] cards for cancer.

TIM: Says he only gets cards for cancer.

BOB: Well, John, your mother has decided to leave it, telling people that you have cancer.

JOHN: Well, I don't any more. I have AIDS.

TIM: Don't strain. I can do it.

BOB: It's something for you to take up with her.

> BOB *pulls out another envelope.*

Now, listen, mate, I was reading your will this morning.

JOHN: Where [*cough*] you get that from?

BOB: Pardon?

TIM: John wants to know where you got his will from?

BOB: [*to* JOHN] It was in the drawer of your desk. I have some concerns. Why is everything going to Tim?

JOHN: Shit. [*Cough*] want to make sure he's all right if I die.

BOB: I didn't get any of that.

TIM: He said he wants to make sure I'm all right if he dies.

BOB: And Tim, is your will set out similarly?

TIM: It is.

BOB: And if John doesn't survive you?

TIM: It goes to my family.

BOB: So if John dies, you inherit his belongings. And then say a month later you die? Everything goes to your family? I don't think that's fair. I would like half. I put John through school and college and I think I deserve it. I made a list this morning. Now, who owns the television and video?

> JOHN *sighs.*

TIM: They're John's.

BOB: What about the car? You don't want it, Tim, do you? With all the stuff going on in your brain?

TIM: They're resolving, Bob. But I'm not going to fight you for it. You can have it.

BOB: And the bed?

TIM: Well, there are things we bought together. Can I have a look?

> BOB *hands* TIM *the list. He blinks to focus on it.*

Yeah, it might be better for John and I to go through the list for you, Bob.

BOB: All right.

TIM: [*reading the list*] Because it looks pretty thorough. CDs and videos. Just trying to think who bought the Vegemite last. Probably you, John.

JOHN: [*to* TIM] It hurts my lungs to laugh.

TIM: [*to* JOHN] Sorry.

BOB: Well, you go through it then.

TIM: [*quietly to* JOHN] And the boy videos? Your family would enjoy *Frisky Pool Party #7* but can mine have *Hung Like A Horse*?

BOB: That's right.

JOHN: [*to* TIM] Stop it.

BOB: Might grab some breakfast then.

TIM: And some little red dots to mark up the apartment.

      JOHN *sniggers.*

BOB: Goodo.

TIM: [*to* JOHN] Sorry.

BOB: Some things are only fair.

JOHN: Tim, it's just Dad being Dad.

TIM: Offensive?

JOHN: Shhh.

      Enter SAM.

BOB: [*to* SAM] Ah, you're the doctor. We met.

SAM: Happy with the news?

BOB: He's worked hard.

SAM: Yes.

JOHN: Very happy.

SAM: Don't strain the voice, John. I can hear you. Now about your lung…

BOB: [*to* JOHN] The lung, John.

SAM: We have a number of options. We can keep up the pleurodesis until it sticks.

TIM: How many times can you do it?

SAM: Pretty well forever, if you can stand the pain. Or we can do nothing, just wait for the inevitable and make you as comfortable as possible. Or we can operate, open you up and sew the holes. You'll be left with reduced lung capacity and there is a chance you won't survive.

      BOB *exhales.* TIM *reaches across and holds* JOHN*'s hand.* JOHN *responds, rub rub rub, pat pat pat, kiss.*

TIM: [*aside*] Rub rub rub, pat pat pat, kiss. Always did that.

SAM: The anaesthetist will assess you. They don't like operating on people with underlying chronic illness. They will rate your risk of failure and I want to warn you, he'll probably rate yours at something like twenty-five per cent.

> BOB *extends his hand to* JOHN *but it lands on* TIM*'s hand.* BOB *doesn't realise.*

JOHN: Chance of failure?
SAM: That's right. Death.
TIM: Oh, is that all?

> *At some point,* BOB *sees that it is both* JOHN *and* TIM *that he is touching. He doesn't shift.*

JOHN: I want to go home to Melbourne this Christmas.
SAM: We'd be aiming to have you home after recovery. Long before Christmas. Take some time to think about it.

> SAM *exits.*

JOHN: We should call Mum.
TIM: [*to* BOB] He wants Mum, your, his Mum.
BOB: I'll call her.

> BOB *moves to make the call.*

JOHN: Should include her in the decision.
TIM: Here we are again, John. The Lord giveth…

> *Enter* LOIS. *She mouths her lines without sound.*

BOB: Hello Lois. It's me.
LOIS: [*unvoiced*] Oh Bob. How is he?

> *As the parents talk,* TIM *and* JOHN *have their own separate conversation.*

JOHN: [*to* TIM] I don't want to do nothing.
BOB: [*to* LOIS] He's here now. We've had good news.
JOHN: [*to* TIM] I don't know how many more lung treatments I can stand.
LOIS: [*unvoiced*] What is it, Bob?
TIM: [*to* JOHN] You don't have to have this operation for me.
BOB: [*to* LOIS] Well, mixed news actually. The cancer's resolved.
JOHN: [*to* TIM] You're talking like I'm dying.
LOIS: [*unvoiced*] Oh.

TIM: [*to* JOHN] You're working so hard.

BOB: [*to* LOIS] But they want to operate for the lung thing and I'll put him on.

JOHN: [*to* TIM] How can I think positively when you're talking at me?

BOB: Here she is, John.

JOHN: Hi Mum.

LOIS: [*unvoiced*] Wonderful news, honey. Feel okay?

JOHN: Not too bad. They're going to operate to sew up the holes in my lungs. It's scary because I have a twenty-five per cent chance of failure.

LOIS: [*unvoiced*] Well?

JOHN: My other option is to not fight and that's not what I'm gonna do, Mum.

LOIS: [*unvoiced*] Yes. Thank you. I want to hear straightaway. You know that. I've been praying.

JOHN: Dad said you only tell people I have cancer.

LOIS: [*unvoiced*] Well, that's true.

JOHN: But it's AIDS-related cancer. I'm not ashamed of what I have.

LOIS: [*unvoiced*] No.

JOHN: I want you to tell people the truth.

LOIS: [*unvoiced*] That's difficult for me, John.

JOHN: Please try for me.

LOIS: [*unvoiced*] That's not what I am ready to do... I don't know if I can be your mother if you insist I tell people.

JOHN: That's a shame.

LOIS: [*unvoiced*] No. It's how I...

JOHN: Yes it is.

LOIS: [*unvoiced*] We don't need to talk about this today. Not now.

> JOHN *chews his lip.*

I love you.

JOHN: Okay. Goodbye.

> BOB *wanders off for breakfast.*

TIM: I can tell from your face...

JOHN: She reckons that if I insist on her telling people, she doesn't know if she can be my mother.

TIM: She doesn't mean it.

JOHN: I know, but it hurts.

TIM: There's still hair from arsehole to breakfast.
JOHN: The chemo's stopping. I don't have cancer.
TIM: It's ratty. Will you let me clipper it?

> TIM *lifts off* JOHN*'s wig to reveal a soft buzz cut.*

◆ ◆ ◆ ◆ ◆

TIM *and* JOHN*'s house.*

Enter PETER. *He is dressed for tennis and finds his racquet.*

PETER: Good to be home? Operation done and won.

> TIM *does not acknowledge him.*

You look tired.
TIM: Look, Peter, I can manage. It's my house. I'm not a cripple.
PETER: You're tired.
TIM: And don't tell me I'm tired.
PETER: Okay. You're snapping and acting irrationally because of the toxo and…
TIM: Get real.
PETER: Well, you may not want my help…
TIM: Fuck off.
PETER: But I know John does. And I'd do anything he asked.
TIM: Yeah, because you're in fuckin' love with him. It's not a three-way relationship, Peter.
PETER: No. It's not. Anyway, I'm going now but, if you do need me, I want you to call. I don't want to be late.

> PETER *heads out.*

TIM: He's been sleeping with his eyes half open.
PETER: That's okay. It's normal.
TIM: His ulcer keeps me up and last night I saw him get bitten in the stomach by the devil. I don't want us to go mad, Peter. I don't want you to say that about us. It's not true. Where would his soul go— trapped inside his madness, or floating free?
PETER: Ask a priest. I'm a nurse. Try and get some sleep, Tim, and I'll be back in the morning.
TIM: Did he vomit again?
PETER: I had to reinsert his tube. Tim, Fairfield's prepared to give me

leave without pay so I can be John's carer. If you want help, if you would like, rather than going back to Melbourne, I could stay... John's talking about going up north.

TIM: If I get like John, if I get like John without John, will you do this for me?

PETER: I don't know if I could do that, Tim. You and I have never had the same... I've never really felt like I fit in with all the theatre people, a bit like John, and it was like that with the uni crowd and— John and I were a bit on the sideline and that was good.

TIM: Did he show you the scar from this latest lung op?

PETER: I saw it in the shower.

TIM: I got this rush of repulsion when the nurse gave John his pre-med. Under the hospital gown, these two skin flaps replaced his bum. Where's my John going? He used to be so physical, playing footy, tennis and jogging.

PETER: Best and Fairest 1976.

TIM: I never slept with Woody.

PETER: Woody? I know.

TIM: You slept with John a few times.

PETER: 1980 was a long time ago. Infatuation has long been replaced.

TIM: You were holding the other end of Woody's uranium banner when I first saw you.

PETER: Did I look pissed off?

TIM: These are strange times. Who would have thought when we were in Young Gays that this is where we'd end up?

PETER: I nursed Lee.

TIM: Lee?

PETER: Lee from uni. He was mates with Woody.

TIM: Oh. Yeah. He gave me a swampwater milkshake at my first Gaysoc meeting.

PETER: I barely recognised him—only when I looked at the name on his file. I went to his funeral. They told the story about him being arrested at the first Mardi Gras. He didn't last long. I can't escape it. Every patient's a friend or a lover of a friend or... If you need me to stay and to travel, call me. And call me if John's tube comes up again.

TIM: Thank you for doing the laundry and stocking the fridge and everything. We laughed because—did you even buy condoms?

PETER: Can't remember them on the list.

TIM: We made love last night. Maybe for the last time.

PETER: It's going to happen, Tim.

TIM: He wanted to be fucked, for me to fuck him.

PETER: You don't have to tell me everything, Tim.

TIM: When he came there wasn't much fluid and that's probably a sign of how sick he is. We hadn't had anal sex since we found out about the virus. Way back, John said, 'That's how we got into this mess in the first place.' Last night, he seduced me and undressed me and I felt just how skinny he's got; rolling around caught up in his tubes. It almost didn't work and I said we didn't have to but he wanted me to fuck him and we persisted and he took me inside him. Then we lay there and then he slept and slept. That was such a gift, giving of himself. If John wants to go on a trip to somewhere warm, we should let him.

PETER: We'll organise it. Byron maybe but if he goes to Noosa and something happens we'll need to get to Sydney. I'll sell my Sleaze Ball tickets. We should drive but not too far and I'll come with you. I think it would allow you guys more time alone and you definitely need someone to drive.

    TIM *nods.*

He cries for you daily, Tim. He is afraid you'll face death alone. I'm going to be late. Dinner's in the fridge.

TIM: [*unvoiced*] Thank you.

    PETER *exits.*

♦ ♦ ♦ ♦ ♦

TIM *and* JOHN*'s living room.*

Enter JOHN *struggling to walk. He has tubes twisted and trailing from his limbs.* TIM *assists* JOHN *and during the scene finds himself operating his lover like a marionette puppet.*

TIM: John? Did you wake up?

JOHN: We have to get the cricket whites! The other team will be here in a minute.

TIM: John, what are you talking about?

JOHN: The Australian cricket team. They're coming on the supply ship.

TIM: Where are we?

JOHN: Christmas Island.

TIM: Oh okay. But John, we're in Rose Bay in Sydney. At our apartment.

JOHN: What about the team?

TIM: It's all right, Johnny. I think we should go to see the doctor.

JOHN: I'm not sick. We went to Coffs Harbour.

TIM: Yeah. We're back. Went on our holiday with Peter. To Byron. I have to go see the doctor and I'd like you to come with me.

JOHN: And we're going to Melbourne for Christmas.

TIM: We'll talk to the doctor about that.

JOHN: We're going home for Christmas.

TIM: Okay, sweetie.

> TIM *walks* JOHN *to his bed.*

♦ ♦ ♦ ♦ ♦

Fairfield Hospital, Melbourne.

Enter a NURSE *in cardboard angel wings and tinsel pushing a breakfast trolley. It is Christmas Day.*

NURSE: [*singing*] 'Joy to the world the Lord is come…'

TIM: You look fabulous.

NURSE: Thank you. Christmas breakfast: fruit muffins, fruit salad, scrambled eggs and a chocky. You're John's lover.

TIM: That's right.

NURSE: He's very sweet. Beautiful eyelashes. Sorry you're here today.

TIM: Don't worry, we'll make it the best Christmas ever.

NURSE: Even though we're not meant to feed visitors, what they don't know can't hurt them.

> *She grabs another breakfast from her trolley.* JOHN *runs his fingers through* TIM*'s hair.*

JOHN: My Timba.

TIM: My John. Time for presents?

> TIM *hands* JOHN *a box wrapped in blue wrapping paper with little silver stars.* JOHN *opens it with* TIM*'s assistance.*

JOHN: Better be fun. Mum just gave me pyjamas.

TIM: It's a stable-table. It's like a tray with a pillow under it so you can eat in front of the teev.

JOHN: Thank you. There's something for you under the bed.

> TIM *opens the present.*

I got Peter to get it for me.

TIM: Oh darling, what on earth is it?

JOHN: It's a document holder for writing. It's got a little motorised clamp that moves up and down when you use the foot pedal.

TIM: It's bizarre.

JOHN: You don't like it.

TIM: It's good, but I don't know if the clamp is all that useful. [*Aside*] You always have to tell the truth, don't you, Timothy?

JOHN: For when you write.

TIM: I should. Might keep me sane.

JOHN: It's wrapped in Essendon colours.

TIM: Always. I like it. I'll use it. I promise. Your first present to me was wrapped in Essendon colours. The card said, 'No longer sweet sixteen, hope the next seventeen are as much fun. I love you. John.'

JOHN: You remember that?

TIM: Maybe I'm paraphrasing but I don't think so. And the present was Bryan Ferry's *Let's Stick Together*.

JOHN: That's *cough*.

TIM: You told me that you'd seen him on *Countdown* and he'd made you feel a bit sweaty.

JOHN: Did I?

TIM: And I remember then you looked around and checked the coast was clear and you snuck in a kiss on the lips. I remember that. And then the bell went and we went to Geography together. You've always outdone me on presents.

JOHN: Yesterday didn't hurt *cough* bit. I was just not here and now *cough* ribs are all bruised *cough* the bloody cardiac massage. I wish I'd *cough*. It *cough* so easy, Timba. Are *cough* okay hearing that?

TIM: No, I'm not ready for you to go.

JOHN: *Cough* said our *cough*byes, haven't we?

> *Silence.* TIM *nods. The actor playing* JOHN *climbs out of bed and walks over to another present. He unwraps it. It contains a puppet of* JOHN. *He walks it to the bed. This puppet will take* JOHN's *place for the remainder of the play.*

TIM: You can't go without me at your side.
JOHN: *Cough.*
TIM: That's the deal.
JOHN: *Cough cough cough.*
TIM: I love you too.

> TIM *kisses the puppet. The actor playing* JOHN *remains on stage.* JOHN*'s breathing underscores the scene. Enter* BOB, *adjusting his glasses to read from a scrap of paper.*

BOB: Nurse said they've given him—I wrote down the names— 'Largactil' to help suppress the cough and the morphine will remove any anxiety. Are you happy with that?
TIM: Yes. Happy with… oh. I see, they'll…[*kill him*]
BOB: Lois is on her way but I think she should sleep tonight. He's decided that he doesn't want to be resuscitated again. He told Lois and the registrar that. He won't let her disobey him.
TIM: Of course he won't. It's John's choice.

> TIM *stares at the puppet. Silence but for the breathing.*

BOB: Just wanted to say, let you know… The funeral is going to be here in Melbourne at a Catholic church. And we don't want anyone making a statement.
TIM: You mean about AIDS?
BOB: That and the gay thing. Everyone already knows now, so there's no need.
TIM: You know that's against John's wishes. Be it on your conscience.
BOB: It's such a tragedy. How did this happen?
TIM: Your son takes it up the arse, Bob.
BOB: Oh well, that'll do it.
TIM: [*aside*] Well, actually, that's not what we said.
BOB: [*again*] It's such a tragedy. How did this happen?
TIM: I'm sorry, Bob, I don't know.
BOB: It's getting on. Lois should sleep tonight. I should too.

> BOB *exits. Night descends.* TIM *holds the puppet. The groaning starts to sound like wailing.* TIM *gently rubs the puppet's hand: rub rub rub, pat pat pat, kiss. The groans calm. Enter* LOIS. *She reaches into her bag and pulls out two salad rolls wrapped in Glad Wrap.*

LOIS: Just salad. I hope that's okay.

TIM: Thank you. That's wonderful.

LOIS: In for the long haul.

TIM: There's that fold-out. You're welcome to sleep on it.

LOIS: Might sit up for a bit. Thank you.

TIM: You've got the time?

LOIS: About one a.m. You probably haven't slept much.

TIM: No. Feeling it. Phoebe and Peter have been great.

> *Silence.* JOHN's *wailing sounds like sex.* LOIS *hears it.* TIM *rubs the puppet and the groaning softens.*

LOIS: Bob and I found a nice grave this morning. Yesterday. It's under a tree, and we're having a boulder as a headstone with a brass plaque on it. Do you like the sound of that?

TIM: I think that's good.

LOIS: And Bob and I are going to be buried with him. We'd like that.

> *Silence.*

You have a sleep if you like.

TIM: Weird, tomorrow's Australia Day.

LOIS: January flies.

TIM: Especially when you're... My sleep's so shallow. Did I sleep then?

LOIS: Think I did. It's near three.

TIM: Don't think I did.

LOIS: John, will you shut up, we're trying to sleep.

> *They laugh.*

TIM: Lois, do you remember the time I was staying at your house and I forgot to bring my school pants?

LOIS: The only pair we had were old ones of Chris'. I'll never forget seeing you walking to the bus in such tight pants with the legs at half-mast.

TIM: I can still hear John's cackle.

LOIS: He was such a good-looking boy.

TIM: It amazes me how beautiful he still is.

LOIS: He is such a gentle soul. This is what I was afraid of; the unknown. He loved you, Tim.

TIM: I hope he knows how loved he is, how many phone calls I get and how many visitors want to come. People who say how unfair it is and how he's the nicest person they have ever known. A lot of tears have been shed for you this week, John.

LOIS: He was my favourite. I shouldn't say it, all my boys are wonderful. But he was my favourite. Never a problem.

> JOHN's *breathing stops momentarily. They sit up.* JOHN *breathes again.*

John, you're tricking us.

TIM: Bob spoke to me about the car, Lois. I said I didn't want it but…

LOIS: You don't have to deal with Bob. You come to me. The car is yours.

> *A morning bird calls. Enter* BOB *with* FATHER WOOD.

FATHER WOOD: You must be Tim. I'm Father Wood, the pastoral-care worker here.

TIM: Pleased to meet you.

FATHER WOOD: Bob and Lois have requested the last rites for John.

> FATHER WOOD *dons a scapular. He makes the sign of the cross on the puppet's forehead with oil from a small bottle, as he reads in priestly tones.*

In the name of the Almighty Father who created you, in the name of Jesus Christ, Son of the living God who suffered for you, in the name of the Holy Spirit who was poured out upon you. Go forth, faithful Christian. May you live in peace this day. May your home be with God in Zion, with Mary the Virgin Mother of God, with Joseph and all the angels and saints. My brother in faith, I entrust you to God who created you and take you from Tim. Tim, this is really happening. Tim, this time tomorrow he will be dead. Tim, no more cuddle bunnies. Tim, no more 'Timba'. Tim, no more feeling. Tim has gone numb. John, in your name, Amen.

> TIM *snaps out of his wandering.*

ALL: Amen.

> FATHER WOOD *exits.* TIM *moves away. Enter* PHOEBE *and* PETER.

TIM: Phoebe? Peter?

PHOEBE: Tim, it's time to come back in.

> JOHN's *groans are loud and amplified.* LOIS, BOB, PETER *and* PHOEBE *surround the puppet of* JOHN. *The actor playing* JOHN *also remains.* TIM *turns to face the scene ahead.*

TIM: [*aside*] Fuck—blind fear—schoolboy about to get the strap— fuck—Bob and Lois holding his hands—Peter and Phoebe at his feet. Fuck—where am I supposed to sit?

> *Silence.* TIM *slides in behind* BOB *and strokes* JOHN*'s head.* BOB *pushes in front of him and kisses* JOHN*'s forehead.*

[*Aside*] His breathing soon shallower—quieter—then—nostrils flare. The sweet smell of faeces in the air—a lot of dignity in death. Still quieter and shallower—and then—saliva bubbles blow.

> BOB *grabs a tissue and wipes the puppet's chin.* JOHN*'s breathing stops.*

[*Heard by* JOHN] You stopped breathing. You're dead.

> *After a moment* PETER *and* TIM *begin washing the puppet body of* JOHN. BOB *crashes around the room putting things into plastic bags.* PETER *takes a tissue and removes the turd sitting between* JOHN*'s legs and places it in a contaminated-waste bin.* LOIS *stares off into the distance.* PHOEBE *thumbs through her address book.* PETER *is concentrating on washing* JOHN*'s feet.* BOB *is focused on clearing the room. Only the actor who played* JOHN *is watching* TIM *as he reaches to the puppet—rub rub rub, pat pat pat, kiss.*

> LOIS *and* PHOEBE *exit. As* BOB *and* PETER *carry off the puppet they recite:*

BOB: *The Melbourne Age*, January 27, 1992.

PETER: *The Sydney Star Observer*, January 30, 1992.

BOB: Caleo, John Robert.

PETER: John Caleo.

BOB: Sleep peacefully, my son, now there's no more pain.

PETER: We won't forget your fighting spirit and your kind and innocent heart.

BOB: You will always be remembered until we meet again.

PETER: Our love and support to Tim Conigrave, John's partner in life for the past fifteen years.

BOB: All our love, Mum, Dad, Michael, Paul, Christopher and Anthony.

◆ ◆ ◆ ◆ ◆

Epilogue.

TIM: Dear John,

I am sitting in the garden at the back of my hotel, surrounded by orange trees and bougainvilleas. After the madness of the northern cities, the island of Lipari is paradise.

I visited the island of Salina yesterday, the island where your grandparents were born. It was a bit like a private pilgrimage. It is almost barren, lots of rock and caper bushes. The café is only open for an hour and you can understand why they emigrated.

The most unnerving thing: here on Lipari there is a beautiful boy who works in the bar in our hotel. He is so like you he could easily be one of your brothers. He was born here but his family is not Caleo. He is so gentle and so shy. We try to talk but he speaks Liparota, a dialect I can't understand. He occupies my dreams: I fall in love so easily these days.

Life is pretty good at the moment: I have my health and seem to be doing most of the things I want to do before I die. I guess the hardest thing is having so much love for you and it somehow not being returned. I develop crushes all the time but that is just misdirected need for you. You are a hole in my life, a black hole.

Anything I place there cannot be returned.

The actor playing JOHN *leaves the stage.*

I miss you terribly. Ci vedremo lassù, angelo.

ACTOR PLAYING TIM: Timothy Conigrave died in October 1994. *Holding the Man* was published in 1995: a gift to John. The End.

THE END